Breakfast with Benedict

Daily Readings

POPE BENEDICT XVI

BREAKFAST WITH BENEDICT

Daily Readings

POPE BENEDICT XVI

EDITED BY BERT GHEZZI

Our Sunday Visitor Publishing Division
Our Sunday Visitor, Inc.
Huntington, Indiana 46750

Copyright © 2009 by Libreria Editrice Vaticana

Copyright © 2009 by Our Sunday Visitor Publishing Division
Our Sunday Visitor, Inc. Published 2009

14 13 12 11 10 09   1 2 3 4 5 6 7 8 9

ISBN 978-1-59276-576-8 (Inventory No. T860)
LCCN: 2009922143

Cover design by Tyler Ottinger
Interior design by Sherri L. Hoffman
Cover and interior photos by Stefano Spaziani

PRINTED IN THE UNITED STATES OF AMERICA

Let us turn our gaze toward Christ.
It is he who will make us free to love as he loves us,
and to build a reconciled world.

— POPE BENEDICT XVI

CONTENTS

*T*his little book creates an opportunity for you to start your day with Pope Benedict XVI. Imagine that you have been invited to breakfast with the pope. As you sip your first cup of coffee, he will talk to you about an important and interesting topic. Today he may reflect with you on the Face of God, one of his favorite themes. Tomorrow he may share about his personal experience of going to Confession. And the next day he may express his concern that we care for the environment. The wide range of his interests and depth of his understanding will fascinate you. His savvy grasp of what's going on in the world will cause you to nod your head in agreement. Some mornings what he says will make you think. On other days he may provoke you to change something in your life. And on most days his words will draw you to prayer.

You may have expected your host to be stodgy, hard-nosed, and defensive. That was the popular, media-driven view of Cardinal Joseph Ratzinger when he served as Prefect of the Congregation for the Doctrine of the Faith. But as you listen to Pope Benedict XVI, you will learn how inaccurate that portrayal was. You will notice his kindness to the poor and marginalized, his gentleness with wrongdoers, his patience with the misguided, and his affection for all.

So take this book with you to your table and enjoy your breakfast with Benedict, our Holy Father.

Bert Ghezzi
All Saints, 2008

Meditations from

POPE BENEDICT XVI

1

SEEING GOD'S LOVE

God has made himself visible; in Jesus we are able to see the Father (cf. Jn 14:9). Indeed, God is visible in a number of ways. In the love story recounted by the Bible, he comes toward us, he seeks to win our hearts, all the way to the Last Supper, to the piercing of his heart on the Cross, to his appearances after the Resurrection, and to the great deeds by which, through the activity of the Apostles, he guided the nascent Church along its path. Nor has the Lord been absent from subsequent Church history; he encounters us ever anew, in the men and women who reflect his presence, in his word, in the sacraments, and especially in the Eucharist. In the Church's Liturgy, in her prayer, in the living community of believers, we experience the love of God, we perceive his presence, and we thus learn to recognize that presence in our daily lives. He has loved us first and he continues to do so; we too, then, can respond with love. God does not demand of us a feeling which we ourselves are incapable of producing. He loves us, he makes us see and experience his love, and since he has "first loved us" (1 Jn 4:19), love can also blossom as a response within us.

DEUS CARITAS EST, 17

2

LIFE IS A RELATIONSHIP

*M*an's great, true hope which holds firm in spite of all disappointments can only be God — God who has loved us and who continues to love us "to the end," until all "is finished" (cf. Jn 13:1 and 19:30). Whoever is moved by love begins to perceive what "life" really is. He begins to perceive the meaning of the word of hope that we encountered in the Baptismal Rite: from faith I await "eternal life" — the true life which, whole and unthreatened, in all its fullness, is simply life. Jesus, who said that he had come so that we might have life and have it in its fullness, in abundance (cf. Jn 10:10), has also explained to us what "life" means: "this is eternal life, that they know you the only true God, and Jesus Christ whom you have sent" (Jn 17:3). Life in its true sense is not something we have exclusively in or from ourselves; it is a relationship. And life in its totality is a relationship with him who is the source of life. If we are in relation with him who does not die, who is Life itself and Love itself, then we are in life. Then we "live."

SPE SALVI, 27

DRAWN NEAR TO GOD

*I*n Jesus, the Heavenly Father inaugurated a new relationship with us; he made us "sons in the Son himself." . . . [I]t is precisely on this reality that St. John invites us to meditate. . . . The beloved Apostle of the Lord stresses that we are really sons: "and so we are" (1 Jn 3:1). We are not only creatures, but we are sons; in this way God is close to us; in this way he draws us to himself at the moment of his Incarnation, in his becoming one of us. Therefore, we truly belong to the family whose Father is God, because Jesus, the Only-Begotten Son, came to pitch his tent among us, the tent of his flesh, to gather all the nations together into a single family, the family of God, belonging to the divine Being united in one people, one family. He came to reveal to us the true Face of the Father, and if we now use the word "God," it is no longer a reality known only from afar. We know the Face of God; it is that of the Son, who came to bring the heavenly realities closer to us and to the earth.

GENERAL AUDIENCE, JANUARY 3, 2007

THE CROSS GIVES US JOY

After affirming, "Whoever would save his life will lose it; and whoever loses his life for my sake and the gospel's will save it," Jesus adds, "For what does it profit a man, to gain the whole world and forfeit his life?" (Mk 8:35-36). To what extent does a life that is totally spent in achieving success, longing for prestige, and seeking commodities to the point of excluding God from one's horizon truly lead to happiness? Can true happiness exist when God is left out of consideration? Experience shows that we are not happy because our material expectations and needs are satisfied. In fact, the only joy that fills the human heart is that which comes from God; indeed, we stand in need of infinite joy. Neither daily concerns nor life's difficulties succeed in extinguishing the joy that is born from friendship with God. Jesus' invitation to take up one's cross and follow him may at first sight seem harsh and contrary to what we hope for, mortifying our desire for personal fulfillment. At a closer look, however, we discover that it is not like this; the witness of the saints shows that in the Cross of Christ, in the love that is given, in renouncing the possession of oneself, one finds that deep serenity which is the source of generous dedication to our brethren, especially to the poor and the needy, and this also gives us joy.

GENERAL AUDIENCE, FEBRUARY 6, 2008

THE HEART OF THE CHRISTIAN FAITH

*G*od is love, and he who abides in love abides in God, and God abides in him" (1 Jn 4:16). These words from the First Letter of John express with remarkable clarity the heart of the Christian faith: the Christian image of God and the resulting image of mankind and its destiny. In the same verse, St. John also offers a kind of summary of the Christian life, "We know and believe the love God has for us."

. . . [I]n these words the Christian can express the fundamental decision of his life. Being Christian is not the result of an ethical choice or a lofty idea, but the encounter with an event, a person, which gives life a new horizon and a decisive direction. St. John's Gospel describes that event in these words, "God so loved the world that he gave his only-begotten Son, that whoever believes in him should . . . have eternal life" (3:16). In acknowledging the centrality of love, Christian faith has retained the core of Israel's faith, while at the same time giving it new depth and breadth. The pious Jew prayed daily the words of the book of Deuteronomy which expressed the heart of his existence: "Hear, O Israel: the LORD our God is one

LORD, and you shall love the LORD your God with all your heart, and with all your soul, and with all your might" (6:4-5). Jesus united into a single precept this commandment of love for God and the commandment of love for neighbor found in the book of Leviticus: "You shall love your neighbor as yourself" (19:18; cf. Mk 12:29-31).

DEUS CARITAS EST, 1

AT THE BEGINNING OF BENEDICT XVI'S PONTIFICATE

Thus, as I prepare myself for the service that is proper to the Successor of Peter, I also wish to confirm my determination to continue to put the Second Vatican Council into practice, following in the footsteps of my Predecessors and in faithful continuity with the 2,000-year tradition of the Church. This very year marks the 40th anniversary of the conclusion of the Council (December 8, 1965). As the years have passed, the conciliar documents have lost none of their timeliness; indeed, their teachings are proving particularly relevant to the new situation of the Church and the current globalized society. My Pontificate begins in a particularly meaningful way as the Church is living the special year dedicated to the Eucharist. How could I fail to see this providential coincidence as an element that must mark the ministry to which I am called? The Eucharist, the heart of Christian life and the source of the Church's evangelizing mission, cannot but constitute the permanent center and source of the Petrine ministry that has been entrusted to me.

FIRST MESSAGE OF HIS HOLINESS BENEDICT XVI, APRIL 20, 2005

THE NAME "BENEDICT"

I wanted to be called Benedict XVI in order to create a spiritual bond with Benedict XV, who steered the Church through the period of turmoil caused by the First World War. He was a courageous and authentic prophet of peace and strove with brave courage first of all to avert the tragedy of the war and then to limit its harmful consequences. Treading in his footsteps, I would like to place my ministry at the service of reconciliation and harmony between persons and peoples, since I am profoundly convinced that the great good of peace is first and foremost a gift of God. . . .

The name "Benedict" also calls to mind the extraordinary figure of the great "Patriarch of Western Monasticism," St. Benedict of Nursia, Co-Patron of Europe together with Sts. Cyril and Methodius and the women saints, Bridget of Sweden, Catherine of Siena, and Edith Stein.

. . . [H]e is a fundamental reference point for European unity and a powerful reminder of the indispensable Christian roots of his culture and civilization.

We are familiar with the recommendation that this Father of Western Monasticism left to his monks in his Rule: "Prefer nothing to the love of Christ" (Rule 72:11; cf. 4:21). At the beginning of my service as Successor of Peter, I ask St. Benedict to help us keep Christ firmly at the heart of our lives. May Christ always have pride of place in our thoughts and in all our activities!

GENERAL AUDIENCE, APRIL 27, 2005

8

THE FOUNDATION OF
ALL REALITY

*T*he Word of God is the foundation of everything, it is the true reality. And to be realistic, we must rely upon this reality. We must change our idea that matter, solid things, things we can touch, are the more solid, the more certain reality. At the end of the Sermon on the Mount, the Lord speaks to us about the two possible foundations for building the house of one's life, sand and rock. The one who builds on sand builds only on visible and tangible things, on success, on career, on money. Apparently these are the true realities. But all this one day will pass away. We can see this now with the fall of large banks; this money disappears, it is nothing. And thus all things, which seem to be the true realities we can count on, are only realities of a secondary order. The one who builds his life on these realities, on matter, on success, on appearances, builds upon sand. Only the Word of God is the foundation of all reality, it is as stable as the heavens and more than the heavens, it is reality. Therefore, we must change our concept of realism. The realist is the one who recognizes the Word of God, in this apparently weak reality, as the foundation of all things. The realist is the one who builds his life on this foundation, which is permanent.

ADDRESS AT THE OPENING OF THE 12TH ORDINARY GENERAL ASSEMBLY OF THE SYNOD OF BISHOPS, OCTOBER 6, 2008

SAVORING THE WORD OF GOD

I urge you to become familiar with the Bible, and to have it at hand so that it can be your compass pointing out the road to follow. By reading it, you will learn to know Christ. Note what St. Jerome said in this regard, "Ignorance of the Scriptures is ignorance of Christ" (PL 24, 17; cf. *Dei Verbum*, 25). A time-honored way to study and savor the word of God is *lectio divina* which constitutes a real and veritable spiritual journey marked out in stages. After the *lectio*, which consists of reading and rereading a passage from Sacred Scripture and taking in the main elements, we proceed to *meditatio*. This is a moment of interior reflection in which the soul turns to God and tries to understand what his word is saying to us today. Then comes *oratio*, in which we linger to talk with God directly. Finally, we come to *contemplatio*. This helps us to keep our hearts attentive to the presence of Christ whose word is "a lamp shining in a dark place, until the day dawns and the morning star rises in your hearts" (2 Pet 1:19). Reading, study, and meditation on the Word should then flow into a life of consistent fidelity to Christ and his teachings.

MESSAGE TO THE YOUTH OF THE WORLD ON THE
OCCASION OF THE 21ST WORLD YOUTH DAY, APRIL 9, 2006

10

THE BREATH OF GOD

*J*ohn's Gospel tells us that after the Resurrection the Lord went to his disciples, breathed upon them, and said, "Receive the Holy Spirit" (Jn 20:22). This is a parallel to Genesis, where God breathes on the mixture he made with the dust from the earth and it comes to life and becomes man. Then man, who is inwardly darkened and half-dead, receives Christ's breath anew and it is this breath of God that gives his life a new dimension that gives him life with the Holy Spirit. We can say, therefore, that the Holy Spirit is the breath of Jesus Christ and we, in a certain sense, must ask Christ to breathe on us always, so that his breath will become alive and strong and work upon the world. This means that we must keep close to Christ. We do so by meditating on his Word. We know that the principal author of the Sacred Scriptures is the Holy Spirit. When, through his Word, we speak with God, when we do not only seek the past in it but truly the Lord who is present and speaks to us, then . . . it is as if we were to find ourselves strolling in the garden of the Holy Spirit; we talk to him and he talks to us. . . . And then, naturally, this listening, walking in the environment of the Word, must be transformed into a response — a response in prayer, in contact with Christ.

MEETING WITH THE CLERGY OF THE
DIOCESE OF BOLZANO-BRESSANONE, AUGUST 6, 2008

PRAYER — HOPE IN ACTION

*W*hat matters most is that you develop your personal relationship with God. That relationship is expressed in prayer. God by his very nature speaks, hears, and replies. Indeed, St. Paul reminds us, we can and should "pray constantly" (1 Thess 5:17). Far from turning in on ourselves or withdrawing from the ups and downs of life, by praying we turn toward God and through him to each other, including the marginalized and those following ways other than God's path (cf. *Spe Salvi*, 33). As the saints teach us so vividly, prayer becomes hope in action. Christ was their constant companion, with whom they conversed at every step of their journey for others.

MEETING WITH YOUNG PEOPLE AND SEMINARIANS
AT SAINT JOSEPH SEMINARY, YONKERS, NEW YORK,
APRIL 19, 2008

12

CONFIDING IN MARY

$\mathcal{A}$t noon, when the first hours of the day are already beginning to weigh us down with fatigue, our availability and our generosity are renewed by the contemplation of Mary's "yes." This clear and unreserved "yes" is rooted in the mystery of Mary's freedom, . . . completely separated from any complicity with sin, thanks to the privilege of her Immaculate Conception. This privilege given to Mary, which sets her apart from our common condition, does not distance her from us, but on the contrary, it brings her closer. While sin divides, separating us from one another, Mary's purity makes her infinitely close to our hearts, attentive to each of us and desirous of our true good. You see it here in Lourdes, as in all Marian shrines; immense crowds come thronging to Mary's feet to entrust to her their most intimate thoughts, their most heartfelt wishes. That which many, either because of embarrassment or modesty, do not confide to their nearest and dearest, they confide to her who is all pure, to her Immaculate Heart — with simplicity, without frills, in truth. . . . The Virgin Mary's maternal love disarms all pride; it renders man capable of seeing himself as he is, and it inspires in him the desire to be converted so as to give glory to God.

ANGELUS, SEPTEMBER 14, 2008

THE GRACE OF HUMBLE SERVICE

*T*he one who serves does not consider himself superior to the one served, however miserable his situation at the moment may be. Christ took the lowest place in the world — the Cross — and by this radical humility he redeemed us and constantly comes to our aid. Those who are in a position to help others will realize that in doing so they themselves receive help; being able to help others is no merit or achievement of their own. This duty is a grace. The more we do for others, the more we understand and can appropriate the words of Christ, "We are unworthy servants" (Lk 17:10). We recognize that we are not acting on the basis of any superiority or greater personal efficiency, but because the Lord has graciously enabled us to do so. There are times when the burden of need and our own limitations might tempt us to become discouraged. But precisely then we are helped by the knowledge that, in the end, we are only instruments in the Lord's hands; and this knowledge frees us from the presumption of thinking that we alone are personally responsible for building a better world. In all humility we will do what we can, and in all humility we will entrust the rest to the Lord. It is God who governs the world, not we.

DEUS CARITAS EST, 35

14

SIGNS OF INFINITE MERCY

*L*et no heart be closed to the omnipotence of [God's] redeeming love! Jesus Christ died and rose for all; he is our hope — true hope for every human being. Today, just as he did with his disciples in Galilee before returning to the Father, the risen Jesus now sends us everywhere as witnesses of his hope, and he reassures us: I am with you always, all days, until the end of the world (cf. Mt 28:20). Fixing the gaze of our spirit on the glorious wounds of his transfigured body, we can understand the meaning and value of suffering, we can tend the many wounds that continue to disfigure humanity in our own day. In his glorious wounds we recognize the indestructible signs of the infinite mercy of the God of whom the prophet says: it is he who heals the wounds of broken hearts, who defends the weak and proclaims the freedom of slaves, who consoles all the afflicted, and bestows upon them the oil of gladness instead of a mourning robe, a song of praise instead of a sorrowful heart (cf. Is 61:1-3). If with humble trust we draw near to him, we encounter in his gaze the response to the deepest longings of our heart: to know God and to establish with him a living relationship in an authentic communion of love, which can fill our lives, our interpersonal and social relations, with that same love. For this reason, humanity needs Christ: in him, our hope, "we were saved" (Rom 8:24).

URBI ET ORBI MESSAGE, EASTER 2008

CARING FOR CREATION

*W*e need to care for the environment; it has been entrusted to men and women to be protected and cultivated with responsible freedom, with the good of all as a constant guiding criterion. Human beings, obviously, are of supreme worth vis-à-vis creation as a whole. Respecting the environment does not mean considering material or animal nature more important than man. Rather, it means not selfishly considering nature to be at the complete disposal of our own interests, for future generations also have the right to reap its benefits and to exhibit toward nature the same responsible freedom that we claim for ourselves. Nor must we overlook the poor, who are excluded in many cases from the goods of creation destined for all. Humanity today is rightly concerned about the ecological balance of tomorrow. It is important for assessments in this regard to be carried out prudently, in dialogue with experts and people of wisdom, uninhibited by ideological pressure to draw hasty conclusions, and above all with the aim of reaching agreement on a model of sustainable development capable of ensuring the well-being of all while respecting environmental balances. If the protection of the environment involves costs, they should be justly distributed, taking due account of the different levels of development of various countries and the need for solidarity with future generations.

MEETING WITH THE BISHOPS OF THE
UNITED STATES OF AMERICA, APRIL 16, 2008

THE WITNESS OF CHRISTIAN COMMUNITY

*I*f we are to understand the mission of the Church, we must go back to the Upper Room where the disciples remained together (cf. Lk 24:49), praying with Mary, the "Mother," awaiting the Spirit that had been promised. This icon of the nascent Church should be a constant source of inspiration for every Christian community. Apostolic and missionary fruitfulness is not principally due to programs and pastoral methods that are cleverly drawn up and "efficient," but is the result of the community's constant prayer (cf. *Evangelii Nuntiandi*, 75). Moreover, for the mission to be effective, communities must be united, that is, they must be "of one heart and soul" (cf. Acts 4:32), and they must be ready to witness to the love and joy that the Holy Spirit instills in the hearts of the faithful (cf. Acts 2:42). The Servant of God John Paul II wrote that, even prior to action, the Church's mission is to witness and to live in a way that shines out to others (cf. *Redemptoris Missio*, 26). Tertullian tells us that this is what happened in the early days of Christianity when pagans were converted on seeing the love that reigned among Christians: "See how they love one another" (cf. *Apology*, 39:7).

MESSAGE TO THE YOUNG PEOPLE OF THE WORLD ON THE OCCASION OF THE 23RD WORLD YOUTH DAY, 2008

BEAUTY, TRUTH, AND LOVE

*I*n Christ the beauty of truth and the beauty of love converge; . . . Christ, who is "the beauty of every beauty," as St. Bonaventure used to say (*Sermones Dominicales,* 1:7), is made present in the hearts of men and women and attracts them to their vocation which is love. It is thanks to this extraordinary magnetic force that reason is drawn from its torpor and opened to the Mystery. Thus, the supreme beauty of God's merciful love is revealed and at the same time, the beauty of the human being who, created in the image of God, is regenerated by grace and destined to eternal glory.

Down the ages Christianity has been communicated and disseminated thanks to the newness of life of persons and communities capable of bearing an incisive witness of love, unity, and joy. This force itself has set a vast number of people in "motion," from generation to generation. Was it not perhaps the beauty born from faith on the saints' faces that spurred so many men and women to follow in their footsteps? . . .

Christ still continues today to make resound in the hearts of so many that "come, follow me" which can decide their destiny. This normally happens through the witness of those who have had a personal experience of Christ's presence. On the faces and in the words of these "new creatures," his light becomes visible and his invitation audible.

MESSAGE TO THE PARTICIPANTS OF THE SECOND
WORLD CONGRESS ON ECCLESIAL MOVEMENTS
AND NEW COMMUNITIES, MAY 22, 2006

SHARING CHRIST

*T*he present moment offers us a providential opportunity to listen once again, with simplicity, purity of heart, and faithfulness to Christ who reminds us that we are not servants but his friends. He instructs us to remain in his love without conforming ourselves to the dictates of this world. Let us not be deaf to his Word. Let us learn from him. Let us imitate his way of life. Let us be sowers of his Word (cf. Mk 3:14; Jn 8:33-36; 15:1-8; 17:14-17). Thus, with our entire life, with the joy of knowing we are loved by Jesus whom we can call our brother, we will be effective instruments so that he may continue to attract everyone with the mercy that sprang from his Cross. Dear brothers and sisters, with docility and power, with the charity that the Holy Spirit has infused into our hearts, I encourage you to share this treasure with others because there is no greater richness than enjoying Christ's friendship and walking by his side. It is worth the effort to dedicate our best energies to this great task, knowing that divine grace precedes us, sustains us, and accompanies us in the fulfillment of our mission.

MESSAGE TO HIS EMINENCE CARDINAL ANTONIO JOSÉ
GONZÁLEZ ZUMÁRRAGA, AUGUST 12, 2008

THE RADIANT POWER OF HOPE

*A*ll serious and upright human conduct is hope in action. This is so first of all in the sense that we thereby strive to realize our lesser and greater hopes, to complete this or that task which is important for our onward journey, or we work toward a brighter and more humane world so as to open doors into the future. Yet our daily efforts in pursuing our own lives and in working for the world's future either tire us or turn into fanaticism, unless we are enlightened by the radiance of the great hope that cannot be destroyed even by small-scale failures or by a breakdown in matters of historic importance. If we cannot hope for more than is effectively attainable at any given time, or more than is promised by political or economic authorities, our lives will soon be without hope. It is important to know that I can always continue to hope, even if in my own life, or the historical period in which I am living, there seems to be nothing left to hope for. Only the great certitude of hope that my own life and history in general, despite all failures, are held firm by the indestructible power of Love, and that this gives them their meaning and importance, only this kind of hope can then give the courage to act and to persevere.

SPE SALVI, 35

THE OPPORTUNITY TO
SEE GOD'S GLORY

How can we not hear, from the very depths of this humanity, at once joyful and anguished, a heart-rending cry for help? It is Christmas: today "the true light that enlightens every man" (Jn 1:9) came into the world. "The Word became flesh and dwelt among us" (Jn 1:14), proclaims the Evangelist John. Today, this very day, Christ comes once more "unto his own," and to those who receive him he gives "the power to become children of God"; in a word, he offers them the opportunity to see God's glory and to share the joy of that Love which became incarnate for us in Bethlehem. Today "our Savior is born to the world," for he knows that even today we need him. Despite humanity's many advances, man has always been the same: a freedom poised between good and evil, between life and death. It is there, in the very depths of his being, in what the Bible calls his "heart," that man always needs to be "saved." And, in this post-modern age, perhaps he needs a Savior all the more, since the society in which he lives has become more complex and the threats to his personal and moral integrity have become more insidious. Who can defend him, if not the One who loves him to the point of sacrificing on the Cross his only-begotten Son as the Savior of the world?

Urbi et Orbi Message, Christmas 2006

MEETING JESUS

*D*o not forget that the Sunday Eucharist is a loving encounter with the Lord that we cannot do without. When you recognize him "at the breaking of bread," like the disciples at Emmaus, you will become his companions. He will help you to grow and to give the best of yourselves. Remember that in the Bread of the Eucharist, Christ is really, totally, and substantially present. It is therefore in the mystery of the Eucharist, at Mass and during silent adoration before the Blessed Sacrament of the altar, that you will meet him in a privileged way. By opening your very being and your whole life under the gaze of Christ, you will not be crushed — quite the contrary: you will discover that you are infinitely loved. You will receive the power that you need in order to build your lives and to make the choices that present themselves to you every day. Before the Lord, in the silence of your hearts, some of you may feel called to follow him in a more radical way in the priesthood or the consecrated life. Do not be afraid to listen to this call and to respond with joy. As I said at the inauguration of my Pontificate, God takes nothing away from those who give themselves to him. On the contrary, he gives them everything. He comes to draw out the best that is in each one of us, so that our lives can truly flourish.

VIDEO MESSAGE TO YOUNG PARTICIPANTS IN THE
49TH INTERNATIONAL EUCHARISTIC CONGRESS,
JUNE 21, 2008

LOVING OTHERS, LOVING GOD

$\mathcal{L}$ove of neighbor is thus shown to be possible in the way proclaimed by the Bible, by Jesus. It consists in the very fact that, in God and with God, I love even the person whom I do not like or even know. This can only take place on the basis of an intimate encounter with God, an encounter which has become a communion of will, even affecting my feelings. Then I learn to look on this other person not simply with my eyes and my feelings, but from the perspective of Jesus Christ. His friend is my friend. Going beyond exterior appearances, I perceive in others an interior desire for a sign of love, of concern. This I can offer them not only through the organizations intended for such purposes, accepting it perhaps as a political necessity. Seeing with the eyes of Christ, I can give to others much more than their outward necessities; I can give them the look of love which they crave. Here we see the necessary interplay between love of God and love of neighbor which the First Letter of John speaks of with such insistence. If I have no contact whatsoever with God in my life, then I cannot see in the other anything more than the other, and I am incapable of seeing in him the image of God. But if in my life I fail completely to heed others, solely out of a desire to be "devout" and to perform my "religious duties," then my relationship with God will also grow arid. It becomes merely "proper," but loveless. Only my readiness to encounter my neighbor and to show him love makes me sensitive to God as well.

DEUS CARITAS EST, 18

FINDING THE WORD IN THE WORDS

$\mathcal{W}$e are always searching for the Word of God. . . . Just reading it does not mean necessarily that we have truly understood the Word of God. The danger is that we only see the human words and do not find the true actor within, the Holy Spirit. We do not find the Word in the words.

In this context St. Augustine recalls the scribes and Pharisees who were consulted by Herod when the Magi arrived. Herod wants to know where the Savior of the world would be born. They know it, they give the correct answer: in Bethlehem. . . . However they do not see reality, they do not know the Savior. . . . This is a great danger as well in our reading of Scripture: we stop at the human words, words form the past, history of the past, and we do not discover the present in the past, the Holy Spirit who speaks to us today in the words from the past. In this way we do not enter the interior movement of the Word, which in human words conceals and which opens the divine words. . . . We must always look for the Word within the words.

Therefore, exegesis, the true reading of Holy Scripture, is not only a literary phenomenon, not only reading a text. . . . It is moving toward the Word of God in the human words. Only by conforming ourselves to the Mystery of God, to the Lord who is the Word . . . can we truly find the Word of God in human words. Let us pray to the Lord that he may help us search the word, not only with our intellect but also with our entire existence.

ADDRESS AT THE OPENING OF THE 12TH ORDINARY GENERAL ASSEMBLY OF THE SYNOD OF BISHOPS, OCTOBER 6, 2008

THE URGENCY OF EVANGELIZATION

*W*hat will become of humanity and creation? Is there hope for the future, or rather, is there a future for humanity? And what will this future be like? The answer to these questions comes to those of us who believe from the Gospel. . . . St. Paul had understood well that only in Christ can humanity find redemption and hope. Therefore, he perceived that the mission was pressing and urgent to proclaim "the promise of the life which is in Christ Jesus" (2 Tim 1:1), "our hope" (1 Tim 1:1), so that all peoples could be co-heirs and co-partners in the promise through the Gospel (cf. Eph 3:6). . . .

It is therefore an urgent duty for everyone to proclaim Christ and his saving message. St. Paul said, "Woe to me if I do not preach the gospel!" (1 Cor 9:16). On the way to Damascus he had experienced and understood that the redemption and the mission are the work of God and his love. Love of Christ led him to travel over the roads of the Roman Empire as a herald, an apostle, a preacher, and a teacher of the Gospel of which he declared himself to be an "ambassador in chains" (Eph 6:20). Divine charity made him "all things to all men, that I might by all means save some" (1 Cor 9:22). By looking at St. Paul's experience, we understand that missionary activity is a response to the love with which God loves us.

MESSAGE FOR THE 82ND WORLD MISSION SUNDAY, MAY 11, 2008

INDIVIDUALISM AND COMMUNITY

*I*n a society which values personal freedom and autonomy, it is easy to lose sight of our dependence on others as well as the responsibilities that we bear toward them. This emphasis on individualism has even affected the Church (cf. *Spe Salvi*, 13-15), giving rise to a form of piety which sometimes emphasizes our private relationship with God at the expense of our calling to be members of a redeemed community. Yet from the beginning, God saw that "it is not good that the man should be alone" (Gen 2:18). We were created as social beings who find fulfillment only in love — for God and for our neighbor. If we are truly to gaze upon him who is the source of our joy, we need to do so as members of the people of God (cf. *Spe Salvi*, 14). If this seems counter-cultural, that is simply further evidence of the urgent need for a renewed evangelization of culture.

MEETING WITH THE BISHOPS OF THE
UNITED STATES OF AMERICA, APRIL 16, 2008

AT THE SERVICE OF PEACE

*I*n view of the risks which humanity is facing in our time, all Catholics in every part of the world have a duty to proclaim and embody ever more fully the "Gospel of Peace", and to show that acknowledgment of the full truth of God is the first, indispensable condition for consolidating the truth of peace. God is Love which saves, a loving Father who wants to see his children look upon one another as brothers and sisters, working responsibly to place their various talents at the service of the common good of the human family. God is the unfailing source of the hope which gives meaning to personal and community life. God, and God alone, brings to fulfillment every work of good and of peace. History has amply demonstrated that declaring war on God in order to eradicate him from human hearts only leads a fearful and impoverished humanity toward decisions which are ultimately futile. This realization must impel believers in Christ to become convincing witnesses of the God who is inseparably truth and love, placing themselves at the service of peace in broad cooperation with other Christians, the followers of other religions and with all men and women of good will.

MESSAGE FOR THE CELEBRATION OF THE
WORLD DAY OF PEACE 2006

MARY, SIGN OF OUR TRANSFIGURATION

*A*s the Second Vatican Council teaches, Mary Most Holy should always be seen in the mystery of Christ and of the Church. In this perspective: "The Mother of Jesus in the glory which she possesses in body and soul in heaven is the image and beginning of the Church as it is to be perfected in the world to come. Likewise she shines forth on earth, until the day of the Lord shall come (cf. 2 Pet 3:10)" (*Lumen Gentium,* n. 68). . . . Mary assumed into Heaven points out to us the final destination of our earthly pilgrimage. She reminds us that our whole being — spirit, soul, and body — is destined for fullness of life; that those who live and die in love of God and of their neighbor will be transfigured in the image of the glorious Body of the Risen Christ; that the Lord will cast down the proud and exalt the humble (cf. Lk 1:51-52). With the mystery of her Assumption Our Lady proclaims this eternally. May you be praised for ever, O Virgin Mary! Pray the Lord for us.

Angelus, August 15, 2008

A CASCADE OF THE SPIRIT

*W*e read in the Acts of the Apostles that the disciples were praying all together in the Upper Room when the Holy Spirit descended upon them powerfully, as wind and as fire. They then began to proclaim in many tongues the Good News of Christ's Resurrection (cf. 2:1-4). This was the "Baptism of the Holy Spirit" which had been foretold by John the Baptist: "I baptize you with water," he said to the crowds, "but he who is coming after me is mightier than I, . . . he will baptize you with the Holy Spirit and with fire" (Mt 3:11). In fact, Jesus' entire mission aimed at giving the Spirit of God to men and women and at baptizing them in his regenerative "bath." This was brought about with his glorification (cf. Jn 7:39), that is, through his death and Resurrection: then the Spirit of God was poured out in superabundance, like a cascade capable of purifying every heart, extinguishing the fire of evil and kindling the flame of divine love in the world.

REGINA CAELI, MAY 11, 2008

CHRIST CHALLENGES
OUR HUMANITY

t Christmas, the Almighty becomes a child and asks for our help and protection. His way of showing that he is God challenges our way of being human. By knocking at our door, he challenges us and our freedom; he calls us to examine how we understand and live our lives. The modern age is often seen as an awakening of reason from its slumbers, humanity's enlightenment after an age of darkness. Yet without the light of Christ, the light of reason is not sufficient to enlighten humanity and the world. For this reason, the words of the Christmas Gospel: "the true light that enlightens every man was coming into this world" (Jn 1:9) resound now more than ever as a proclamation of salvation. . . .

Men and women of today, humanity come of age yet often still so frail in mind and will, let the Child of Bethlehem take you by the hand! Do not fear; put your trust in him! The life-giving power of his light is an incentive for building a new world order based on just ethical and economic relationships. May his love guide every people on earth and strengthen their common consciousness of being a "family" called to foster relationships of trust and mutual support. A united humanity will be able to confront the many troubling problems of the present time: from the menace of terrorism to the humiliating poverty in which millions of human beings live, from the proliferation of weapons to the pandemics and the environmental destruction which threatens the future of our planet.

Urbi et Orbi Message, Christmas 2005

EXPANDING OUR CAPACITY FOR GOD

*S*t. Augustine . . . describes very beautifully the intimate relationship between prayer and hope. He defines prayer as an exercise of desire. Man was created for greatness — for God himself; he was created to be filled by God. But his heart is too small for the greatness to which it is destined. It must be stretched. . . . He then uses a very beautiful image to describe this process of enlargement and preparation of the human heart. "Suppose that God wishes to fill you with honey [a symbol of God's tenderness and goodness]; but if you are full of vinegar, where will you put the honey?" The vessel, that is your heart, must first be enlarged and then cleansed, freed from the vinegar and its taste. This requires hard work and is painful, but in this way alone do we become suited to that for which we are destined. Even if Augustine speaks directly only of our capacity for God, it is nevertheless clear that through this effort by which we are freed from vinegar and the taste of vinegar, not only are we made free for God, but we also become open to others. It is only by becoming children of God, that we can be with our common Father. To pray is not to step outside history and withdraw to our own private corner of happiness. When we pray properly we undergo a process of inner purification which opens us up to God and thus to our fellow human beings as well.

SPE SALVI, 33

COMMUNICATING THE TRUTH

*M*an thirsts for truth, he seeks truth; this fact is illustrated by the attention and the success achieved by so many publications, programs, or quality fiction in which the truth, beauty, and greatness of the person, including the religious dimension of the person, are acknowledged and favorably presented. Jesus said: "You will know the truth, and the truth will make you free" (Jn 8:32). The truth which makes us free is Christ, because only he can respond fully to the thirst for life and love that is present in the human heart. Those who have encountered him and have enthusiastically welcomed his message experience the irrepressible desire to share and communicate this truth. As St. John writes, "That which was from the beginning, which we have heard, which we have seen with our eyes, which we have looked upon and touched with our hands, concerning the word of life . . . we proclaim also to you, so that you may have fellowship with us; and our fellowship is with the Father and with his Son Jesus Christ. And we are writing this that our joy may be complete" (1 Jn 1:1-3).

MESSAGE TO THE 42ND WORLD COMMUNICATIONS DAY,
MAY 4, 2008

GOD'S TEMPLE

*S*t. Paul . . . knows well and makes us all understand that the Church is not his and is not ours: the Church is the Body of Christ, it is a Church of God, "God's field, God's building. . . . God's temple" (1 Cor 3:9, 16). This latter designation is particularly interesting because it attributes to a fabric of interpersonal relations a term that commonly served to mean a physical place, considered sacred. The relationship between church and temple therefore comes to assume two complementary dimensions: on the one hand the characteristic of separateness and purity that the sacred building deserved is applied to the ecclesial community, but on the other, the concept of a material space is also overcome, to transfer this quality to the reality of a living community of faith. If previously temples had been considered places of God's presence, it was now known and seen that God does not dwell in buildings made of stone but that the place of God's presence in the world is the living community of believers.

GENERAL AUDIENCE, OCTOBER 15, 2008

TASTE AND SEE

*I*f it is true that the sacraments are part of the Church's pil-grimage through history toward the full manifestation of the victory of the risen Christ, it is also true that, especially in the liturgy of the Eucharist, they give us a real foretaste of the eschatological fulfillment for which every human being and all creation are destined (cf. Rom 8:19ff.). Man is created for that true and eternal happiness which only God's love can give. But our wounded freedom would go astray were it not already able to experience something of that future fulfillment. Moreover, to move forward in the right direction, we all need to be guided toward our final goal. That goal is Christ himself, the Lord who conquered sin and death, and who makes himself present to us in a special way in the eucharistic celebration. Even though we remain "aliens and exiles" in this world (1 Pet 2:11), through faith we already share in the fullness of risen life. The eucharistic banquet, by disclosing its powerful eschatological dimension, comes to the aid of our freedom as we continue our journey.

SACRAMENTUM CARITATIS, 30

LOVE GROWS THROUGH LOVE

*O*nly if I serve my neighbor can my eyes be opened to what God does for me and how much he loves me. The saints — consider the example of Blessed Teresa of Calcutta — constantly renewed their capacity for love of neighbor from their encounter with the Eucharistic Lord, and conversely this encounter acquired its realism and depth in their service to others. Love of God and love of neighbor are thus inseparable, they form a single commandment. But both live from the love of God who has loved us first. No longer is it a question, then, of a "commandment" imposed from without and calling for the impossible, but rather of a freely-bestowed experience of love from within, a love which by its very nature must then be shared with others. Love grows through love. Love is "divine" because it comes from God and unites us to God; through this unifying process it makes us a "we" which transcends our divisions and makes us one, until in the end God is "every thing to every one" (1 Cor 15:28).

DEUS CARITAS EST, 18

FAITH AND HUMAN FULFILLMENT

*I*f we live with Christ we will also succeed in human things. Indeed, faith does not only involve a supernatural aspect, it rebuilds man, bringing him back to his humanity . . . : it is based precisely on the natural virtues: honesty, joy, the willingness to listen to one's neighbor, the ability to forgive, generosity, goodness, and cordiality among people. These human virtues show that faith is truly present, that we are truly with Christ, and I believe that we should pay great attention to this, also regarding ourselves: to develop an authentic humanity in ourselves because faith involves the complete fulfillment of the human being, of humanity. We should pay attention to carrying out human tasks well and correctly, also in our profession, in respect for our neighbor, in being concerned about our neighbor, which is the best way to be concerned about ourselves: in fact, "existing" for our neighbor is the best way of "existing" for ourselves. And the latter subsequently gives rise to those initiatives that cannot be programmed: communities of prayer, communities that read the Bible together or that even provide effective help for people in need, who require it, who are on the margins of life, for the sick, for the disabled, and many other things. This is when our eyes are opened to see our personal skills, to assume the corresponding initiatives and to be able to imbue others with the courage to do the same. And precisely these human things can strengthen us, in a certain way putting us in touch anew with God's Spirit.

MEETING WITH THE CLERGY OF THE
DIOCESE OF BOLZANO-BRESSANONE, AUGUST 6, 2008

COMFORTER OF THE AFFLICTED

*T*he presence of many sick pilgrims at Lourdes, and of the volunteers who accompany them, helps us to reflect on the maternal and tender care that the Virgin expresses toward human pain and suffering. Associated with the Sacrifice of Christ, Mary, *Mater Dolorosa,* who at the foot of the Cross suffers with her divine Son, is felt to be especially near by the Christian community, which gathers around its suffering members who bear the signs of the passion of the Lord. Mary suffers with those who are in affliction, with them she hopes, and she is their comfort, supporting them with her maternal help. And is it not perhaps true that the spiritual experience of very many sick people leads us to understand increasingly that "the Divine Redeemer wishes to penetrate the soul of every sufferer through the heart of his holy Mother, the first and the most exalted of all the redeemed?" (John Paul II, *Salvifici Doloris,* n. 26).

MESSAGE FOR THE 16TH WORLD DAY
OF THE SICK, JANUARY 11, 2008

AN EVENT OF LOVE

*T*hrough the death and resurrection of Christ, we too rise to new life today, and uniting our voice with his, we proclaim that we wish to remain for ever with God, our infinitely good and merciful Father.

In this way we enter the depths of the Paschal mystery. The astonishing event of the resurrection of Jesus is essentially an event of love: the Father's love in handing over his Son for the salvation of the world; the Son's love in abandoning himself to the Father's will for us all; the Spirit's love in raising Jesus from the dead in his transfigured body. And there is more: the Father's love which "newly embraces" the Son, enfolding him in glory; the Son's love returning to the Father in the power of the Spirit, robed in our transfigured humanity. From today's solemnity, in which we relive the absolute, once-and-for-all experience of Jesus' resurrection, we receive an appeal to be converted to Love; we receive an invitation to live by rejecting hatred and selfishness, and to follow with docility in the footsteps of the Lamb that was slain for our salvation, to imitate the Redeemer who is "gentle and lowly in heart," who is "rest for our souls" (cf. Mt 11:29).

URBI ET ORBI MESSAGE, EASTER 2008

MERCY, THE FACE OF GOD

*D*uring the Jubilee of the Year 2000 the beloved Servant of God John Paul II established that throughout the Church the Sunday after Easter should be called . . . Divine Mercy Sunday. This occurred contemporaneously with the canonization of Faustina Kowalska, a humble Polish Sister who was born in 1905 and died in 1938, a zealous messenger of the Merciful Jesus. Indeed, mercy is the central nucleus of the Gospel message; it is the very name of God, the Face with which he revealed himself in the Old Covenant and fully in Jesus Christ, the incarnation of creative and redemptive Love. May this merciful love also shine on the face of the Church and show itself through the sacraments, in particular that of Reconciliation, and in works of charity, both communitarian and individual. May all that the Church says and does manifest the mercy God feels for man, and therefore for us. When the Church has to recall an unrecognized truth or a betrayed good, she always does so impelled by merciful love, so that men and women may have life and have it abundantly (cf. Jn 10:10). From divine mercy, which brings peace to hearts, genuine peace flows into the world, peace between different peoples, cultures, and religions.

REGINA CAELI, MARCH 30, 2008

PRAYING FOR CHRISTIAN UNITY

*I*n the face of difficulties and divisions, Christians cannot be resigned nor yield to discouragement. The Lord asks this of us: to persevere in prayer in order to keep alive the flame of faith, love, and hope which nourishes the desire for full unity. "*Ut unum sint!*," says the Lord. May Christ's invitation always resound in our hearts, . . . Let us give thanks to the Lord for the goals reached in ecumenical dialogue thanks to the Holy Spirit's action; let us be docile, listening to his voice so that our hearts, filled with hope, may continuously seek the path that leads to the full communion of all Christ's disciples.

In his Letter to the Galatians, St. Paul recalls that "the fruit of the Spirit is love, joy, peace, patience, kindness, goodness, faithfulness, gentleness, self-control" (Gal 5:22-23). These are the gifts of the Holy Spirit that we also implore today for all Christians, so that in the common and generous service to the Gospel, they may be a sign of God's love for humanity in the world. Let us turn our gaze confidently to Mary, the Shrine of the Holy Spirit and through her pray, "Come, Holy Spirit, fill the hearts of your faithful and kindle in them the fire of your love." Amen.

GENERAL AUDIENCE, MAY 7, 2008

DOING GOD'S WORK

*Y*ou may remember that when I addressed the crowd in St. Peter's Square on the day of my election it came naturally to me to introduce myself as a laborer in the vineyard of the Lord. Well, in today's Gospel (cf. Mt 20:1-16), Jesus recounted the very same parable of the owner of the vineyard who at different hours of the day hires laborers to work in it. And in the evening he gives them all the same wages, one *denarius*, provoking protests from those who began work early. That *denarius* clearly represents eternal life, a gift that God reserves for all. Indeed those who are considered the "last," if they accept, become the "first," whereas the "first" can risk becoming the "last." The first message of this parable is inherent in the very fact that the landowner does not tolerate, as it were, unemployment: he wants everyone to be employed in his vineyard. Actually, being called is already the first reward: to be able to work in the Lord's vineyard, to put oneself at his service, to collaborate in his work, is in itself a priceless recompense that repays every effort. Yet only those who love the Lord and his Kingdom understand this: those who instead work only for the pay will never realize the value of this inestimable treasure.

ANGELUS, SEPTEMBER 21, 2008

JESUS IS THE ANSWER

$\mathcal{M}$any young people today lack hope. They are perplexed by the questions that present themselves ever more urgently in a confusing world, and they are often uncertain which way to turn for answers. They see poverty and injustice and they long to find solutions. They are challenged by the arguments of those who deny the existence of God and they wonder how to respond. They see great damage done to the natural environment through human greed and they struggle to find ways to live in greater harmony with nature and with one another.

Where can we look for answers? The Spirit points us toward the way that leads to life, to love, and to truth. The Spirit points us toward Jesus Christ. There is a saying attributed to St. Augustine: "If you wish to remain young, seek Christ." In him we find the answers that we are seeking, we find the goals that are truly worth living for, we find the strength to pursue the path that will bring about a better world. Our hearts find no rest until they rest in the Lord, as St. Augustine says at the beginning of the *Confessions*, the famous account of his own youth. My prayer is that the hearts of the young people who gather in Sydney for the celebration of World Youth Day will truly find rest in the Lord, and that they will be filled with joy and fervor for spreading the Good News among their friends, their families, and all whom they meet.

MESSAGE TO THE YOUNG PILGRIMS TAKING PART
IN WORLD YOUTH DAY 2008

LOVE FOR THE POOR IS LITURGY

*P*erhaps we are no longer able to understand fully the meaning that Paul and his communities attributed to the collection for the poor of Jerusalem. It was a completely new initiative in the area of religious activities: it was not obligatory, but free and spontaneous; all the Churches that were founded by Paul in the West took part. The collection expressed the community's debt to the mother Church of Palestine, from which they had received the ineffable gift of the Gospel. The value that Paul attributes to this gesture of sharing is so great that he seldom calls it merely a "collection." Rather, for him it is "service," "blessing," "gift," "grace," even "liturgy" (cf. 2 Cor 9). Particularly surprising is the latter term which gives a value that is even religious to a collection of money: on the one hand it is a liturgical act or "service" offered by every community to God and on the other, it is a loving action made for people. Love for the poor and the divine liturgy go hand in hand, love for the poor is liturgy. The two horizons are present in every liturgy that is celebrated and experienced in the Church which, by her nature, is opposed to any separation between worship and life, between faith and works, between prayer and charity for the brethren.

GENERAL AUDIENCE, OCTOBER 1, 2008

STANDING WITH THE TERMINALLY ILL

*T*he Church, following the example of the Good Samaritan, has always shown particular concern for the infirm. Through her individual members and institutions, she continues to stand alongside the suffering and to attend the dying, striving to preserve their dignity at these significant moments of human existence. Many such individuals — health care professionals, pastoral agents, and volunteers — and institutions throughout the world are tirelessly serving the sick, in hospitals and in palliative care units, on city streets, in housing projects and parishes.

I now turn to you, my dear brothers and sisters suffering from incurable and terminal diseases. I encourage you to contemplate the sufferings of Christ crucified, and, in union with him, to turn to the Father with complete trust that all life, and your lives in particular, are in his hands. Trust that your sufferings, united to those of Christ, will prove fruitful for the needs of the Church and the world. I ask the Lord to strengthen your faith in his love, especially during these trials that you are experiencing. It is my hope that, wherever you are, you will always find the spiritual encouragement and strength needed to nourish your faith and bring you closer to the Father of Life. Through her priests and pastoral workers, the Church wishes to assist you and stand at your side, helping you in your hour of need, and thus making present Christ's own loving mercy toward those who suffer.

MESSAGE FOR THE 16TH WORLD DAY OF THE SICK,
JANUARY 11, 2008

WELCOMING THE HOLY SPIRIT

*T*he Holy Spirit continues today to act with power in the Church, and the fruits of the Spirit are abundant in the measure in which we are ready to open up to this power that makes all things new. For this reason it is important that each one of us know the Spirit, establish a relationship with Him, and allow ourselves to be guided by Him. . . . In our profession of faith we proclaim: "I believe in the Holy Spirit, the Lord and giver of life, who proceeds from the Father and the Son" (Nicene-Constantinopolitan Creed). Yes, the Holy Spirit, the Spirit of the love of the Father and of the Son, is the Source of life that makes us holy, "because God's love has been poured into our hearts through the Holy Spirit which has been given to us" (Rom 5:5). Nevertheless, it is not enough to know the Spirit; we must welcome Him as the guide of our souls, as the "Teacher of the interior life" who introduces us to the Mystery of the Trinity, because He alone can open us up to faith and allow us to live it each day to the full. The Spirit impels us forward toward others, enkindles in us the fire of love, makes us missionaries of God's charity.

. . . Indeed, remember that it is precisely the presence of the Spirit within us that confirms, constitutes, and builds our person on the very Person of Jesus crucified and risen.

MESSAGE TO THE YOUNG PEOPLE OF THE WORLD ON THE OCCASION OF THE 23RD WORLD YOUTH DAY, 2008

MARY, GATE OF HEAVEN

*W*hat does the human person in every epoch need other than this: a firm anchorage in life? Here once again is the wonderful meaning of Mary's presence among us. Turning our gaze to her, like the first disciples, we are immediately directed to the reality of Jesus: the Mother points to the Son who is no longer physically among us but awaits us in the Father's house. Jesus invites us not to linger looking upwards, but to be united in prayer together, to invoke the gift of the Holy Spirit. Indeed, only those who are "born from on high," that is, from God's Spirit, have access to the Kingdom of Heaven (cf. Jn 3:3-5), and the first to be "born from on high" was, precisely, the Virgin Mary. To her, therefore, let us turn in the fullness of Easter joy.

REGINA CAELI, MAY 4, 2008

LISTENING TO GOD

*T*here is another aspect of prayer which we need to remember: silent contemplation. St. John, for example, tells us that to embrace God's revelation we must first listen, then respond by proclaiming what we have heard and seen (cf. 1 Jn 1:2-3; *Dei Verbum*, 1). Have we perhaps lost something of the art of listening? Do you leave space to hear God's whisper, calling you forth into goodness? Friends, do not be afraid of silence or stillness, listen to God, adore him in the Eucharist. Let his word shape your journey as an unfolding of holiness.

MEETING WITH YOUNG PEOPLE AND SEMINARIANS
AT SAINT JOSEPH SEMINARY, YONKERS, NEW YORK,
APRIL 19, 2008

SPREADING THE KINGDOM

*I*n the experience of the Apostle to the Gentiles, whom the Lord called to be a "minister of the Gospel," vocation and mission are inseparable. He therefore represents a model for every Christian, particularly for missionaries *ad vitam,* in other words, those men and women who dedicate themselves totally to proclaiming Christ to those who still do not know him, a vocation which has retained its full value. This missionary service is carried out in the first place by priests who dispense the Word of God and the sacraments and who manifest the healing presence of Jesus Christ to all, especially the sick, the lowly, and the poor through their charitable Apostolate. . . . Let us pray that the ranks of those who decide to live the Gospel radically with the vows of chastity, poverty, and obedience may be ever more numerous. They are men and women who have a primary role in evangelization. Some of them are dedicated to contemplation and prayer, others to a multi-faceted educational and charitable action, but they all have the same goal in common: to witness to God's primacy over everything and to spread his Kingdom in every social milieu. . . . Finally, it should not be forgotten that the vocation to Christian marriage is a missionary vocation: indeed, the spouses are called to live the Gospel in families, in work contexts, in parish and in civil communities. In some cases they also offer their valuable collaboration to the mission *ad gentes*.

Regina Caeli, April 13, 2008

OPEN TO ALL

$\mathcal{I}$n reading the Acts of the Apostles and the letters that Paul addressed to various recipients, we perceive a model of a Church that was not exclusive but on the contrary open to all, formed by believers without distinction of culture or race: every baptized person is, in fact, a living member of the one Body of Christ. In this perspective, fraternal solidarity expressed in daily gestures of sharing, joint participation, and joyful concern for others, acquires a unique prominence. However, it is impossible to achieve this dimension of brotherly mutual acceptance, St. Paul always teaches, without the readiness to listen to and welcome the Word preached and practiced (cf. 1 Thess 1:6), a Word that urges all to be imitators of Christ (cf. Eph 5:1-2), to be imitators of the Apostle (cf. 1 Cor 11:1). And therefore, the more closely the community is united to Christ, the more it cares for its neighbor, eschewing judgment, scorn, and scandal, and opening itself to reciprocal acceptance (cf. Rom 14:1-3; 15:7). Conformed to Christ, believers feel they are "brothers" in him, sons of the same Father (cf. Rom 8:14-16; Gal 3:26; 4:6). This treasure of brotherhood makes them "practice hospitality" (Rom 12:13), which is the firstborn daughter of *agape* (cf. 1 Tim 3:2, 5:10; Tit 1:8; Philem 17).

MESSAGE FOR THE 95TH WORLD DAY
OF MIGRANTS AND REFUGEES, 2009

A HOUSECLEANING
FOR THE SOUL

[Although] it is not necessary to go to confession before each Communion, it is very helpful to confess with a certain regularity. It is true: our sins are always the same, but we clean our homes, our rooms, at least once a week, even if the dirt is always the same; in order to live in cleanliness, in order to start again. Otherwise, the dirt might not be seen but it builds up. Something similar can be said about the soul, for me myself: if I never go to confession, my soul is neglected, and in the end I am always pleased with myself and no longer understand that I must always work hard to improve, that I must make progress. And this cleansing of the soul which Jesus gives us in the Sacrament of Confession helps us to make our consciences more alert, more open, and hence, it also helps us to mature spiritually and as human persons. Therefore, two things: confession is only necessary in the case of a serious sin, but it is very helpful to confess regularly in order to foster the cleanliness and beauty of the soul and to mature day by day in life.

CATECHETICAL MEETING WITH CHILDREN WHO HAD RECEIVED THEIR FIRST COMMUNION DURING THE YEAR, OCTOBER 15, 2005

THE TRUE NATURE OF LOVE

Eros and *agape* — ascending love and descending love — can never be completely separated. The more the two, in their different aspects, find a proper unity in the one reality of love, the more the true nature of love in general is realized. Even if *eros* is at first mainly covetous and ascending, a fascination for the great promise of happiness, in drawing near to the other, it is less and less concerned with itself, increasingly seeks the happiness of the other, is concerned more and more with the beloved, bestows itself, and wants to "be there for" the other. The element of *agape* thus enters into this love, for otherwise *eros* is impoverished and even loses its own nature. On the other hand, man cannot live by oblative, descending love alone. He cannot always give, he must also receive. Anyone who wishes to give love must also receive love as a gift. Certainly, as the Lord tells us, one can become a source from which rivers of living water flow (cf. Jn 7:37-38). Yet to become such a source, one must constantly drink anew from the original source, which is Jesus Christ, from whose pierced heart flows the love of God (cf. Jn 19:34).

DEUS CARITAS EST, 7

EARLY CATHOLIC
SOCIAL DOCTRINE

*S*t. John Chrysostom proposed in his continuing *Commentary on the Acts of the Apostles* the model of the primitive Church (cf. Acts 4:32-37) as a pattern for society, developing a social "utopia." . . . In fact, it was a question of giving the city a soul and a Christian face. . . . Chrysostom realized that it is not enough to give alms, to help the poor sporadically, but it is necessary to create a new structure, a new model of society; a model based on the outlook of the New Testament. It was this new society that was revealed in the newborn Church. John Chrysostom thus truly became one of the great Fathers of the Church's social doctrine: the old idea of the Greek *polis* gave way to the new idea of a city inspired by Christian faith. With Paul (cf. 1 Cor 8:11), Chrysostom upheld the primacy of the individual Christian, of the person as such, even of the slave and the poor person. His project thus corrected the traditional Greek vision of the *polis*, the city in which large sectors of the population had no access to the rights of citizenship while in the Christian city all are brothers and sisters with equal rights. The primacy of the person is also a consequence of the fact that it is truly by starting with the person that the city is built, whereas in the Greek *polis* the homeland took precedence over the individual who was totally subordinated to the city as a whole. So it was that a society built on the Christian conscience came into being with Chrysostom.

General Audience, September 26, 2007

THE WORK OF THE HOLY SPIRIT

*O*nly Christ can fulfill the most intimate aspirations that are in the heart of each person. Only Christ can humanize humanity and lead it to its "divinization." Through the power of his Spirit he instills divine charity within us, and this makes us capable of loving our neighbor and ready to be of service. The Holy Spirit enlightens us, revealing Christ crucified and risen, and shows us how to become more like Him so that we can be "the image and instrument of the love which flows from Christ" (*Deus Caritas Est,* 33). Those who allow themselves to be led by the Spirit understand that placing oneself at the service of the Gospel is not an optional extra, because they are aware of the urgency of transmitting this Good News to others. Nevertheless, we need to be reminded again that we can be witnesses of Christ only if we allow ourselves to be led by the Holy Spirit who is "the principal agent of evangelization" (cf. *Evangelii Nuntiandi*, 75) and "the principal agent of mission" (cf. *Redemptoris Missio*, 21).

MESSAGE TO THE YOUNG PEOPLE OF THE WORLD ON THE OCCASION OF THE 23RD WORLD YOUTH DAY, 2008

HOPE FOR THE WORLD'S HEALING

*S*uffering is a part of our human existence. Suffering stems partly from our finitude, and partly from the mass of sin which has accumulated over the course of history and continues to grow unabated today. Certainly we must do whatever we can to reduce suffering: to avoid as far as possible the suffering of the innocent; to soothe pain; to give assistance in overcoming mental suffering. These are obligations both in justice and in love, and they are included among the fundamental requirements of the Christian life and every truly human life. . . . Indeed, we must do all we can to overcome suffering, but to banish it from the world altogether is not in our power. This is simply because we are unable to shake off our finitude and because none of us is capable of eliminating the power of evil, of sin which, as we plainly see, is a constant source of suffering. Only God is able to do this: only a God who personally enters history by making himself man and suffering within history. We know that this God exists, and hence that this power to take "away the sin of the world" (Jn 1:29) is present in the world. Through faith in the existence of this power, hope for the world's healing has emerged in history. It is, however, hope — not yet fulfillment; hope that gives us the courage to place ourselves on the side of good even in seemingly hopeless situations, aware that, as far as the external course of history is concerned, the power of sin will continue to be a terrible presence.

SPE SALVI, 36

BELIEF IN THE DIVINITY OF JESUS

*T*he famous hymn contained in the Letter to the Philippians (cf. 2:6-11) . . . is one of the most elevated texts in the whole of the New Testament. The vast majority of exegetes today agree that this passage reproduces an earlier composition than the text of the Letter to the Philippians. This is a very important fact because it means that Judaeo-Christianity, prior to St. Paul, believed in Jesus' divinity. In other words, faith in the divinity of Jesus was not a Hellenistic invention that emerged much later than Jesus' earthly life, an invention which, forgetful of his humanity, would have divinized him; we see in reality that early Judaeo-Christianity believed in the divinity of Jesus. Indeed, we can say that the Apostles themselves, at the important moments in the life of their Teacher, understood that he was the Son of God, as St. Peter said in Caesarea Philippi: "You are the Christ, the Son of the living God" (Mt 16:16).

GENERAL AUDIENCE, OCTOBER 22, 2008

THE FAMILY OF GOD

*I*n his Letter to Timothy, Paul describes the Church as the "household of God" (1 Tim 3:15); and this is a truly original definition because it refers to the Church as a community structure in which warm, family-type interpersonal relations are lived. The Apostle helps us to understand ever more deeply the mystery of the Church in her different dimensions as an assembly of God in the world. This is the greatness of the Church and the greatness of our call; we are a temple of God in the world, a place in which God truly dwells, and at the same time we are a community, a family of God who is love. As a family and home of God, we must practice God's love in the world and thus, with the power that comes from faith, be a place and a sign of his presence. Let us pray the Lord to grant us to be increasingly his Church, his Body, the place where his love is present in this world of ours and in our history.

GENERAL AUDIENCE, OCTOBER 15, 2008

NOURISHED BY THE SACRAMENTS

*Y*ou might ask, how can we allow ourselves to be renewed by the Holy Spirit and to grow in our spiritual lives? The answer, as you know, is this: we can do so by means of the Sacraments, because faith is born and is strengthened within us through the Sacraments, particularly those of Christian initiation: Baptism, Confirmation, and the Eucharist, which are complementary and inseparable (cf. *Catechism of the Catholic Church*, 1285). This truth concerning the three Sacraments that initiate our lives as Christians is perhaps neglected in the faith life of many Christians. They view them as events that took place in the past and have no real significance for today, like roots that lack life-giving nourishment. It happens that many young people distance themselves from their life of faith after they have received Confirmation. There are also young people who have not even received this sacrament. Yet it is through the sacraments of Baptism, Confirmation, and then, in an ongoing way, the Eucharist, that the Holy Spirit makes us children of the Father, brothers and sisters of Jesus, members of his Church, capable of a true witness to the Gospel, and able to savor the joy of faith.

MESSAGE TO THE YOUNG PEOPLE OF THE WORLD ON THE OCCASION OF THE 23RD WORLD YOUTH DAY, 2008

NO HALF MEASURES

*T*he key to every hope is found in love, solely in authentic love, because love is rooted in God. We read in the Bible: "We know and believe the love God has for us. God is love" (1 Jn 4:16). And God's love has the sweet and compassionate Face of Jesus Christ. Here then we have reached the heart of the Christian message: Christ is the response to your questions and problems; in him every honest aspiration of the human being is strengthened. Christ, however, is demanding and shuns half measures. He knows he can count on your generosity and coherence; for this reason he expects a lot of you. Follow him faithfully and, in order to encounter him, love his Church, feel responsible, do not avoid being courageous protagonists, each in his own context. Here is a point to which I would like to call your attention: seek to know the Church, to understand and love her, paying attention to the voice of her Pastors. She is made up of human beings, but Christ is her head and his Spirit firmly guides her. You are the youthful face of the Church so do not fail to make your contribution in order that the Gospel she proclaims may spread everywhere. Be apostles of your peers!

PASTORAL VISIT TO THE LOCAL POPULATION AND THE YOUNG PEOPLE
OF SANTA MARIA DI LEUCA AND BRINDISI, JUNE 14, 2008

CONQUERING RACISM

*T*he universality of the mission of the Church . . . is made up of people of every race and culture. From precisely this stems the great responsibility of the ecclesial community which is called to be a hospitable home for all, a sign and instrument of communion for the entire human family. How important it is, especially in our time, that every Christian community increasingly deepens its awareness of this in order also to help civil society overcome every possible temptation to give into racism, intolerance, and exclusion and to make decisions that respect the dignity of every human being! One of humanity's great achievements is in fact its triumph over racism. However, unfortunately disturbing new forms of racism are being manifested in various countries. They are often related to social and economic problems which can, however, never justify contempt and racial discrimination. Let us pray that respect for every person everywhere will increase, together with a responsible awareness that only in the reciprocal acceptance of one and all is it possible to build a world distinguished by authentic justice and true peace.

ANGELUS, AUGUST 17, 2008

MARY'S FUNDAMENTAL TITLE

The description "Mother of God" . . . is . . . the fundamental name with which the Community of Believers has always honored the Blessed Virgin. It clearly explains Mary's mission in salvation history. All other titles attributed to Our Lady are based on her vocation to be the Mother of the Redeemer, the human creature chosen by God to bring about the plan of salvation, centered on the great mystery of the Incarnation of the Divine Word

Let us think of the privilege of the "Immaculate Conception," that is, of Mary being immune to sin from conception: she was preserved from any stain of sin because she was to be the Mother of the Redeemer. The same applies to the title "Our Lady of the Assumption": the One who had brought forth the Savior could not be subject to the corruption that derives from original sin. And we know that all these privileges were not granted in order to distance Mary from us but, on the contrary, to bring her close; indeed, since she was totally with God, this woman is very close to us and helps us as a mother and a sister. The unique and unrepeatable position that Mary occupies in the Community of Believers also stems from her fundamental vocation to being Mother of the Redeemer. Precisely as such, Mary is also Mother of the Mystical Body of Christ, which is the Church.

General Audience, January 2, 2008

A LIGHT SHINING IN THE DARKNESS

*M*ay the light of Christ, which comes to enlighten every human being, shine forth and bring consolation to those who live in the darkness of poverty, injustice, and war; to those who are still denied their legitimate aspirations for a more secure existence, for health, education, stable employment, for fuller participation in civil and political responsibilities, free from oppression and protected from conditions that offend against human dignity. It is the most vulnerable members of society — women, children, the elderly — who are so often the victims of brutal armed conflicts, terrorism, and violence of every kind, which inflict such terrible sufferings on entire populations. . . . Throughout the world the number of migrants, refugees, and evacuees is also increasing because of frequent natural disasters, often caused by alarming environmental upheavals.

May the Child Jesus bring relief to those who are suffering, and may he bestow upon political leaders the wisdom and courage to seek and find humane, just, and lasting solutions. To the thirst for meaning and value so characteristic of today's world, to the search for prosperity and peace that marks the lives of all mankind, to the hopes of the poor: Christ — true God and true Man — responds with his Nativity. Neither individuals nor nations should be afraid to recognize and welcome him: with him "a shining light" brightens the horizon of humanity; in him "a holy day" dawns that knows no sunset.

URBI ET ORBI MESSAGE, CHRISTMAS 2007

BROTHERS AND SISTERS OF THE "FIRST-BORN"

*I*n [St. Paul's Letter to the Colossians], Christ is described as the "first-born of all creation" (1:15-20). This word "first-born" suggests that the first of numerous children, the first of a great many brothers and sisters, came down to draw us and make us his brothers and sisters. In the Letter to the Ephesians we find a beautiful exposition of the divine plan of salvation, when Paul says that in Christ God desired to recapitulate everything (cf. Eph 1:23). Christ is the epitome of all things, he takes everything upon himself and guides us to God. And thus he involves us in a movement of descent and ascent, inviting us to share in his humility, that is, in his love for neighbor, in order also to share in his glorification, becoming with him sons in the Son. Let us pray the Lord to help us conform to his humility, to his love, in order to be rendered participants in his divinization.

GENERAL AUDIENCE, OCTOBER 22, 2008

PRAYER STRENGTHENS ACTION

When we consider the immensity of others' needs, we can, on the one hand, be driven toward an ideology that would aim at doing what God's governance of the world apparently cannot: fully resolving every problem. Or we can be tempted to give in to inertia, since it would seem that in any event nothing can be accomplished. At such times, a living relationship with Christ is decisive if we are to keep on the right path, without falling into an arrogant contempt for man, something not only unconstructive but actually destructive, or surrendering to a resignation which would prevent us from being guided by love in the service of others. Prayer, as a means of drawing ever new strength from Christ, is concretely and urgently needed. People who pray are not wasting their time, even though the situation appears desperate and seems to call for action alone. Piety does not undermine the struggle against the poverty of our neighbors, however extreme. In the example of Blessed Teresa of Calcutta we have a clear illustration of the fact that time devoted to God in prayer not only does not detract from effective and loving service to our neighbor but is in fact the inexhaustible source of that service. In her letter for Lent 1996, Blessed Teresa wrote to her lay co-workers: "We need this deep connection with God in our daily life. How can we obtain it? By prayer."

Deus Caritas Est, 36

THREATENING NUCLEAR CLOUDS

Another disturbing issue is the desire recently shown by some states to acquire nuclear weapons. This has heightened even more the widespread climate of uncertainty and fear of a possible atomic catastrophe. We are brought back in time to the profound anxieties of the "cold war" period. When it came to an end, there was hope that the atomic peril had been definitively overcome and that mankind could finally breathe a lasting sigh of relief. How timely, in this regard, is the warning of the Second Vatican Council that "every act of war directed to the indiscriminate destruction of whole cities or vast areas with their inhabitants is a crime against God and humanity, which merits firm and unequivocal condemnation." Unfortunately, threatening clouds continue to gather on humanity's horizon. The way to ensure a future of peace for everyone is found not only in international accords for the non-proliferation of nuclear weapons, but also in the determined commitment to seek their reduction and definitive dismantling. May every attempt be made to arrive through negotiation at the attainment of these objectives! The fate of the whole human family is at stake!

MESSAGE FOR THE CELEBRATION OF THE
WORLD DAY OF PEACE 2006

LET'S TURN OUR GAZE TOWARD CHRIST

*T*he sign of the Cross is a kind of synthesis of our faith, for it tells how much God loves us; it tells us that there is a love in this world that is stronger than death, stronger than our weaknesses and sins. . . . It is this mystery of the universality of God's love for men that Mary came to reveal here, in Lourdes. She invites all people of good will, all those who suffer in heart or body, to raise their eyes toward the Cross of Jesus, so as to discover there the source of life, the source of salvation. The Church has received the mission of showing all people this loving face of God, manifested in Jesus Christ. Are we able to understand that in the Crucified One of Golgotha, our dignity as children of God, tarnished by sin, is restored to us? Let us turn our gaze toward Christ. It is he who will make us free to love as he loves us, and to build a reconciled world. For on this Cross, Jesus took upon himself the weight of all the sufferings and injustices of our humanity. He bore the humiliation and the discrimination, the torture suffered in many parts of the world by so many of our brothers and sisters for love of Christ. We entrust all this to Mary, mother of Jesus and our mother, present at the foot of the Cross.

HOMILY, SEPTEMBER 14, 2008

THE ORIGIN OF "CHURCH"

Today I would like to speak about St. Paul's teaching on the Church. We must start by noting that this word, *Chiesa* in Italian, as in French *Église*, and in Spanish *Iglesia*, comes from the Greek *ekklesia*. It comes from the Old Testament and means the assembly of the People of Israel, convoked by God. . . . This word now means the new community of believers in Christ who feel that they are God's assembly, the new convocation of all the peoples by God and before him. The term *ekklesia* comes only from the pen of Paul. . . . It makes its first appearance in the greeting of his First Letter to the Thessalonians, where Paul textually addresses "the Church of the Thessalonians" (cf. also "the Church of the Laodiceans" in Col 4:16). In other letters, he speaks of the Church of God which is at Corinth (1 Cor 1:2; 2 Cor 1:1) and of the churches of Galatia (Gal 1:2, etc.), particular churches therefore, but he also says he persecuted "the Church of God" — not a specific local community, but "the Church of God." Thus we see that this word, "Church," has a multi-dimensional meaning: it indicates a part of God's assembly in a specific place (a city, a country, a house) but it also means the Church as a whole. And thus we see that "the Church of God" is not only a collection of various local Churches but that these various local Churches in turn make up one Church of God.

GENERAL AUDIENCE, OCTOBER 15, 2008

THE GRACES OF CONFIRMATION

*C*onfirmation gives us *special strength* to witness to and glorify God with our whole lives (cf. Rom 12:1). It makes us intimately aware of our belonging to the Church, the "Body of Christ," of which we are all living members, in solidarity with one another (cf. 1 Cor 12:12-25). By allowing themselves to be guided by the Spirit, each baptized person can bring his or her own contribution to the building up of the Church because of the *charisms* given by the Spirit, for "to *each* is given the manifestation of the Spirit for the *common good*" (1 Cor 12:7, emphasis added). When the Spirit acts, he brings his fruits to the soul, namely "love, joy, peace, patience, kindness, goodness, faithfulness, gentleness, self-control" (Gal 5:22). To those of you who have not yet received the sacrament of Confirmation, I extend a cordial invitation to prepare to receive it, and to seek help from your priests. It is a special occasion of grace that the Lord is offering you. Do not miss this opportunity!

MESSAGE TO THE YOUNG PEOPLE OF THE WORLD ON THE
OCCASION OF THE 23RD WORLD YOUTH DAY, 2008

REACHING OUT TO THE VULNERABLE

*W*hat happens when people, especially the most vulnerable, encounter a clenched fist of repression or manipulation rather than a hand of hope? A first group of examples pertains to the heart. Here, the dreams and longings that young people pursue can so easily be shattered or destroyed. I am thinking of those affected by drug and substance abuse, homelessness and poverty, racism, violence, and degradation — especially of girls and women. While the causes of these problems are complex, all have in common a poisoned attitude of mind which results in people being treated as mere objects — a callousness of heart takes hold which first ignores, then ridicules, the God-given dignity of every human being. Such tragedies also point to what might have been and what could be, were there other hands — your hands — reaching out. I encourage you to invite others, especially the vulnerable and the innocent, to join you along the way of goodness and hope.

MEETING WITH YOUNG PEOPLE AND SEMINARIANS
AT SAINT JOSEPH SEMINARY, YONKERS, NEW YORK, APRIL 19, 2008

MARY'S SMILE

*T*he psalmist . . . prophesies regarding the Virgin Mary that the richest of the people will seek her smile (cf. Ps 45:12-13). In this way, prompted by the inspired word of Scripture, Christians have always sought the smile of Our Lady, this smile which medieval artists were able to represent with such marvelous skill. . . .

This smile of Mary is for all; but it is directed quite particularly to those who suffer, so that they can find comfort and solace therein. To seek Mary's smile is not an act of devotional or outmoded sentimentality, but rather the proper expression of the living and profoundly human relationship which binds us to her whom Christ gave us as our Mother.

To wish to contemplate this smile of the Virgin does not mean letting oneself be led by an uncontrolled imagination. Scripture itself discloses it to us through the lips of Mary when she sings the Magnificat: "My soul magnifies the Lord, and my spirit rejoices in God my Savior" (Lk 1:46-47). When the Virgin Mary gives thanks to the Lord, she calls us to witness. Mary shares, as if by anticipation, with us, her future children, the joy that dwells in her heart, so that it can become ours. Every time we recite the Magnificat, we become witnesses of her smile. Here in Lourdes, in the course of the apparition of Wednesday, March 3, 1858, Bernadette contemplated this smile of Mary in a most particular way. It was the first response that the Beautiful Lady gave to the young visionary who wanted to know who she was.

HOMILY, SEPTEMBER 15, 2008

INVITATION TO CONVERSION

[On Ash Wednesday] as he places the ashes on the person's forehead the celebrant says "Remember you are dust, and to dust you shall return" (cf. Gen 3:19), or he repeats Jesus' exhortation "Repent, and believe in the Gospel" (cf. Mk 1:15). Both formulas are a reminder of the truth about human life: we are limited creatures, sinners always in need of repentance and conversion. How important it is to listen to and accept this reminder in our time! When contemporary man proclaims his total autonomy from God, he enslaves himself and often finds himself in comfortless loneliness. The invitation to conversion, therefore, is an incentive to return to the embrace of God, the tender and merciful Father, to entrust oneself to him, to entrust oneself to him as adoptive sons, regenerated by his love. With wise pedagogy the Church repeats that conversion is first and foremost a grace, a gift that opens the heart to God's infinite goodness. He himself anticipates with his grace our desire for conversion and accompanies our efforts for full adherence to his saving will. Therefore, to convert is to let oneself be won over by Jesus (cf. Phil 3:12) and "to return" with him to the Father.

GENERAL AUDIENCE, FEBRUARY 6, 2008

THE AIM OF ALL CREATION

The history of salvation is not a small event, on a poor planet, in the immensity of the universe. It is not a minimal thing which happens by chance on a lost planet. It is the motive for everything, the motive for creation. Everything is created so that this story can exist, the encounter between God and his creature. In this sense, salvation history, the Covenant, precedes creation. During the Hellenistic period, Judaism developed the idea that the Torah would have preceded the creation of the material world. This material world seems to have been created solely to make room for the Torah, for this Word of God that creates the answer and becomes the history of love. The mystery of Christ already is mysteriously revealed here. This is what we are told in the Letter to the Ephesians and to the Colossians: Christ is the *protòtypos,* the first-born of creation, the idea for which the universe was conceived. He welcomes all. We enter in the movement of the universe by uniting with Christ. One can say that, while material creation is the condition for the history of salvation, the history of the Covenant is the true cause of the cosmos. We reach the roots of being by reaching the mystery of Christ, his living word that is the aim of all creation.

ADDRESS AT THE OPENING OF THE 12TH ORDINARY
GENERAL ASSEMBLY OF THE SYNOD OF BISHOPS,
OCTOBER 6, 2008

THE CROSS, THE EUCHARIST, AND THE CHURCH

*T*hrough the sacrament of the Eucharist Jesus draws the faithful into his "hour;" he shows us the bond that he willed to establish between himself and us, between his own person and the Church. Indeed, in the sacrifice of the Cross, Christ gave birth to the Church as his Bride and his Body. The Fathers of the Church often meditated on the relationship between Eve's coming forth from the side of Adam as he slept (cf. Gen 2:21-23) and the coming forth of the new Eve, the Church, from the open side of Christ sleeping in death: from Christ's pierced side, John recounts, there came forth blood and water (cf. Jn 19:34), the symbol of the sacrament. A contemplative gaze "on him whom they have pierced" (Jn 19:37) leads us to reflect on the causal connection between Christ's sacrifice, the Eucharist, and the Church. . . . The Church is able to celebrate and adore the mystery of Christ present in the Eucharist precisely because Christ first gave himself to her in the sacrifice of the Cross.

SACRAMENTUM CARITATIS, **14**

THE CREATIVE FORCE
OF LOVE

*T*hose who pray never lose hope, even when they find themselves in a difficult and even humanly hopeless plight. Sacred Scripture teaches us this and Church history bears witness to this.

In fact, how many examples we could cite of situations in which it was precisely prayer that sustained the journey of saints and of the Christian people! Among the testimonies of our epoch I would like to mention the examples of two saints whom we are commemorating in these days: Teresa Benedicta of the Cross, Edith Stein, whose feast we celebrated on August 9, and Maximilian Mary Kolbe, whom we will commemorate . . . , on August 14. . . . Both ended their earthly life with martyrdom in the concentration camp of Auschwitz. Their lives might seem to have been a defeat, but it is precisely in their martyrdom that the brightness of Love which dispels the gloom of selfishness and hatred shines forth. The following words are attributed to St. Maximilian Kolbe, who is said to have spoken them when the Nazi persecution was raging: "Hatred is not a creative force: it is love alone." And heroic proof of his love was the generous offering he made of himself in exchange for a fellow prisoner, an offer that culminated in his death in the starvation bunker on August 14, 1941.

GENERAL AUDIENCE, AUGUST 13, 2008

GOD'S CALL

Friends, again I ask you, what about today? What are you seeking? What is God whispering to you? The hope which never disappoints is Jesus Christ. The saints show us the selfless love of his way. As disciples of Christ, their extraordinary journeys unfolded within the community of hope, which is the Church. It is from within the Church that you too will find the courage and support to walk the way of the Lord. Nourished by personal prayer, prompted in silence, shaped by the Church's liturgy you will discover the particular vocation God has for you. Embrace it with joy. You are Christ's disciples today. Shine his light upon this great city and beyond. Show the world the reason for the hope that resonates within you. Tell others about the truth that sets you free.

MEETING WITH YOUNG PEOPLE AND SEMINARIANS
AT SAINT JOSEPH SEMINARY, YONKERS, NEW YORK,
APRIL 19, 2008

THE REALITY OF THE LIVING JESUS

*S*t. Paul did not think of Jesus in historical terms, as a person of the past. He certainly knew the great tradition of the life, words, death, and Resurrection of Jesus, but does not treat all this as something from the past; he presents it as the reality of the living Jesus. For Paul, Jesus' words and actions do not belong to the historical period, to the past. Jesus is alive now, he speaks to us now and lives for us. This is the true way to know Jesus and to understand the tradition about him. We must also learn to know Jesus not from the human point of view, as a person of the past, but as our Lord and Brother, who is with us today and shows us how to live and how to die.

GENERAL AUDIENCE, OCTOBER 8, 2008

SEEKING TRUTH AND FREEDOM

*H*ave you noticed how often the call for freedom is made without ever referring to the truth of the human person? Some today argue that respect for freedom of the individual makes it wrong to seek truth, including the truth about what is good. In some circles to speak of truth is seen as controversial or divisive, and consequently best kept in the private sphere. And in truth's place — or better said its absence — an idea has spread which, in giving value to everything indiscriminately, claims to assure freedom and to liberate conscience. This we call relativism. But what purpose has a "freedom" which, in disregarding truth, pursues what is false or wrong? How many young people have been offered a hand which in the name of freedom or experience has led them to addiction, to moral or intellectual confusion, to hurt, to a loss of self-respect, even to despair and so tragically and sadly to the taking of their own life? Dear friends, truth is not an imposition. Nor is it simply a set of rules. It is a discovery of the One who never fails us; the One whom we can always trust. In seeking truth we come to live by belief because ultimately truth is a person: Jesus Christ. That is why authentic freedom is not an opting out. It is an opting in; nothing less than letting go of self and allowing oneself to be drawn into Christ's very being for others (cf. *Spe Salvi*, 28).

MEETING WITH YOUNG PEOPLE AND SEMINARIANS
AT SAINT JOSEPH SEMINARY, YONKERS, NEW YORK,
APRIL 19, 2008

THE BODY OF CHRIST

[St. Paul originated the concept of the Church] as the "Body of Christ." . . . It is necessary to bear in mind the two dimensions of this concept. One is sociological in character, according to which the body is made up of its elements and would not exist without them. This interpretation appears in the Letter to the Romans and in the First Letter to the Corinthians, in which Paul uses an image that already existed in Roman sociology: he says that a people is like a body with its different parts, each of which has its own function but all together, even its smallest and seemingly most insignificant parts are necessary if this body is to be able to live and carry out its functions. The Apostle appropriately observes that in the Church there are many vocations: prophets, apostles, teachers, simple people, all are called to practice charity every day, all are necessary in order to build the living unity of this spiritual organism. The other interpretation refers to the actual Body of Christ. Paul holds that the Church is not only an organism but really becomes the Body of Christ in the Sacrament of the Eucharist, where we all receive his Body and really become his Body. Thus is brought about the spousal mystery that all become one body and one spirit in Christ. So it is that the reality goes far beyond any sociological image, expressing its real, profound essence, that is, the oneness of all the baptized in Christ, considered by the Apostle "one" in Christ, conformed to the Sacrament of his Body.

GENERAL AUDIENCE, OCTOBER 15, 2008

TRANSFORMING SECULARISM

*W*hile it is true that this country is marked by a genuinely religious spirit, the subtle influence of secularism can nevertheless color the way people allow their faith to influence their behavior. Is it consistent to profess our beliefs in church on Sunday, and then during the week to promote business practices or medical procedures contrary to those beliefs? Is it consistent for practicing Catholics to ignore or exploit the poor and the marginalized, to promote sexual behavior contrary to Catholic moral teaching, or to adopt positions that contradict the right to life of every human being from conception to natural death? Any tendency to treat religion as a private matter must be resisted. Only when their faith permeates every aspect of their lives do Christians become truly open to the transforming power of the Gospel.

MEETING WITH THE BISHOPS OF THE
UNITED STATES OF AMERICA,
APRIL 16, 2008

SEEING PROMOTES BELIEVING

*I*n our cultural context it is not easy to encounter Christ, the Christian life, and the faith life.

Young people require so much guidance if they are truly to find this path. . . . They must realize that living the faith in our time is possible, that it is not a question of something obsolete but rather, that it is possible to live as Christians today and so to find true goodness.

I remember an autobiographical detail in St. Cyprian's writings. "I lived in this world of ours," he says, "totally cut off from God. . . . And in seeing Christians I thought: it is an impossible life, this cannot be done in our world! Then, however, meeting some of them, joining their company, and letting myself be guided in the catechumenate, in this process of conversion to God, I gradually understood: it is possible! And now I am happy at having found life. I have realized that the other was not life, and to tell the truth," he confesses, "even beforehand, I knew that that was not true life."

It seems to me to be very important that the young find people — both of their own age and older — in whom they can see that Christian life today is possible, and also reasonable and feasible.

LENTEN MEETING WITH THE CLERGY OF ROME,
FEBRUARY 22, 2007

INTERPRETING SCRIPTURE

As the Second Vatican Council teaches in the Constitution *Dei Verbum* (n. 12), a good biblical exegesis demands both the historical-critical and theological methods since Sacred Scripture is the Word of God in human words. This means that every text must be read and interpreted keeping in mind the unity of the whole of Scripture, the living tradition of the Church, and the light of the faith. If it is true that the Bible is also a literary work — even the great codex of universal culture — it is also true that it should not be stripped of the divine element but must be read in the same Spirit in which it was composed. Scientific exegesis and *lectio divina* are therefore both necessary and complementary in order to seek, through the literal meaning, the spiritual meaning that God wants to communicate to us today.

ANGELUS, OCTOBER 26, 2008

BUILT UP IN LOVE

The Real Presence of Christ makes each one of us his "house," and all together we form his Church, the spiritual building of which St. Peter speaks. "Come to him, to that living stone, rejected by men but in God's sight chosen and precious"; the Apostle writes, "and like living stones be yourselves built into a spiritual house, to be a holy priesthood, to offer spiritual sacrifices acceptable to God through Jesus Christ" (1 Pet 2:4-5). St. Augustine remarks, developing, as it were, this beautiful metaphor that through faith people are like the wood and stones collected in the forests and on the mountains for building; then through Baptism, catechesis, and preaching they are rough-shaped, squared, and polished; but they become houses of the Lord only when they are put together with love. When believers are interconnected in accordance with a specific order, mutually close and cohesive, when they are joined by love, they truly become a dwelling of God that is in no danger of collapsing (cf. *Serm.*, 336).

HOMILY, SEPTEMBER 21, 2008

WELCOMING CHRIST THE HEALER

Christ imparts his salvation by means of the sacraments and, especially in the case of those suffering from sickness or disability, by means of the grace of the sacrament of the sick. For each individual, suffering is always something alien. It can never be tamed. That is why it is hard to bear, and harder still . . . to welcome it as a significant element in our vocation, or to accept, as Bernadette expressed it, to "suffer everything in silence in order to please Jesus." To be able to say that, it is necessary to have traveled a long way already in union with Jesus. Here and now, though, it is possible to entrust oneself to God's mercy, as manifested through the grace of the sacrament of the sick. Bernadette herself, in the course of a life that was often marked by sickness, received this sacrament four times. The grace of this sacrament consists in welcoming Christ the healer into ourselves. However, Christ is not a healer in the manner of the world. In order to heal us, he does not remain outside the suffering that is experienced; he eases it by coming to dwell within the one stricken by illness, to bear it and live it with him. Christ's presence comes to break the isolation which pain induces. Man no longer bears his burden alone: as a suffering member of Christ, he is conformed to Christ in his self-offering to the Father, and he participates, in him, in the coming to birth of the new creation.

HOMILY, SEPTEMBER 15, 2008

THE EXEMPLARY CHARITY
OF THE SAINTS

$\mathscr{L}$et us consider the saints, who exercised charity in an exemplary way. Our thoughts turn especially to Martin of Tours (d. 397), the soldier who became a monk and a bishop: he is almost like an icon, illustrating the irreplaceable value of the individual testimony to charity. At the gates of Amiens, Martin gave half of his cloak to a poor man: Jesus himself, that night, appeared to him in a dream wearing that cloak, confirming the permanent validity of the Gospel saying: "I was naked and you clothed me . . ." (Mt 25:36). Yet in the history of the Church, how many other testimonies to charity could be quoted! In particular, the entire monastic movement, from its origins with St. Anthony the Abbot (d. 356), expresses an immense service of charity toward neighbor. In his encounter "face to face" with the God who is Love, the monk senses the impelling need to transform his whole life into service of neighbor, in addition to service of God. This . . . explains the immense initiatives of human welfare and Christian formation, aimed above all at the very poor, who became the object of care firstly for the monastic and mendicant orders, and later for the various male and female religious institutes all through the history of the Church. The figures of saints such as Francis of Assisi, Ignatius of Loyola, John of God, Camillus of Lellis, Vincent de Paul, Louise de Marillac, Giuseppe B. Cottolengo, John Bosco, Luigi Orione, Teresa of Calcutta to name but a few — stand out as lasting models of social charity for all people of good will.

DEUS CARITAS EST, 40

THE POWER OF LIES

*W*ho and what, then, can prevent the coming of peace? Sacred Scripture, in its very first book, Genesis, points to the lie told at the very beginning of history by the animal with a forked tongue, whom the Evangelist John calls "the father of lies" (Jn 8:44). Lying is also one of the sins spoken of in the final chapter of the last book of the Bible, Revelation, which bars liars from the heavenly Jerusalem: "outside are . . . everyone who loves and practices falsehood" (22:15). Lying is linked to the tragedy of sin and its perverse consequences, which have had, and continue to have, devastating effects on the lives of individuals and nations. We need but think of the events of the past century, when aberrant ideological and political systems willfully twisted the truth and brought about the exploitation and murder of an appalling number of men and women, wiping out entire families and communities. After experiences like these, how can we fail to be seriously concerned about lies in our own time, lies which are the framework for menacing scenarios of death in many parts of the world. Any authentic search for peace must begin with the realization that the problem of truth and untruth is the concern of every man and woman; it is decisive for the peaceful future of our planet.

Peace is an irrepressible yearning present in the heart of each person, regardless of his or her particular cultural identity. Consequently, everyone should feel committed to service of this great good, and should strive to prevent any form of untruth from poisoning relationships.

MESSAGE FOR THE CELEBRATION OF THE
WORLD DAY OF PEACE 2006

REMEMBERING
POPE JOHN PAUL I

*J*ohn Paul I chose as his episcopal motto the same motto as St. Charles Borromeo, namely: *Humilitas.* This single word sums up the essential of Christian life and indicates the indispensable virtue of those in the Church who are called to the service of authority. At one of the four General Audiences held during his extremely short Pontificate, he said, among other things, with that familiar tone that distinguished him: "I will just recommend one virtue so dear to the Lord. He said, 'Learn from me who am meek and humble of heart.'. . . Even if you have done great things, say: 'We are useless servants.'" And he observed: "On the contrary the tendency in all of us, is rather the opposite: to show off" (General Audience, September 6, 1978). Humility can be considered his spiritual testament.

Because of this virtue of his, it only took 33 days for Pope Luciani to win people's hearts. "We must feel small before God," he said during the same Audience. And he added, "I am not ashamed to feel like a child before his mother; one believes in one's mother; I believe in the Lord, in what he has revealed to me" (ibid.). These words reveal the full depth of his faith. As we thank God for having given him to the Church and to the world, let us treasure his example, striving to cultivate his same humility which enabled him to talk to everyone, especially the small and the "distant."

ANGELUS, SEPTEMBER 28, 2008

THE SPIRIT OF UNITY
IN DIVERSITY

*J*esus assured his disciples of the help of the Holy Spirit that he would send to continue to make them aware of his presence (cf. Jn 14:16-17). This promise became reality when, after the Resurrection, Jesus entered the Upper Room, greeted the disciples with the words, "Peace be with you," and breathing on them said, "Receive the Holy Spirit" (Jn 20: 22). He authorized them to forgive sins. Here, therefore, the Holy Spirit, appears as a power for the forgiveness of sins, for renewing our hearts and our lives; and thus he renews the earth and creates unity where there was division. Furthermore, on the Feast of Pentecost the Holy Spirit showed himself in other signs: in the sign of a mighty wind, tongues of fire, and the Apostles' ability to speak all languages. This was a sign that the Babylonian dispersion, the result of pride that separates men and women, had been overcome in the Spirit who is love and gives unity in diversity. Since the very first moment of her existence the Church has spoken in all languages — thanks to the power of the Holy Spirit and the tongues of fire — and has lived in all cultures, she does not destroy any of the various gifts, of the different charisms, but draws all of them together in a great, new unity that reconciles: unity and multiformity.

General Audience, May 7, 2008

THE LIGHT OF THE WORLD

"God is light," says St. John, "and in him is no darkness at all" (1 Jn 1:5). In the book of Genesis we read that when the universe was created, "the earth was without form and void, and darkness was upon the face of the deep; . . . And God said, 'Let there be light'; and there was light." (Gen 1:2-3). The creative Word of God is Light, the source of life. All things were made through the Logos, not one thing had its being but through him (cf. Jn 1:3). That is why all creatures are fundamentally good and bear within themselves the stamp of God, a spark of his light. Nevertheless, when Jesus was born of the Virgin Mary, the Light himself came into the world: in the words of the Creed, "God from God, Light from Light." In Jesus, God assumed what he was not, while remaining what he was: "omnipotence entered an infant's body and did not cease to govern the universe" (cf. St. Augustine, *Sermo* 184, No. 1 on Christmas). The Creator of man became man in order to bring peace to the world. For this reason, during Christmas night, the hosts of angels sing: "Glory to God in the highest, and on earth peace among men with whom he is pleased" (Lk 2:14).

Urbi et Orbi Message, Christmas 2007

THE FOLLY OF THE CROSS

*M*any of you wear a cross on a chain around your neck. I too wear one, as every Bishop does. . . . It is the precious symbol of our faith, the visible and material sign that we belong to Christ. St. Paul explains the meaning of the Cross at the beginning of his First Letter to the Corinthians. The Christian community in Corinth was . . . exposed to the corrupting influences of the surrounding culture. Those dangers are similar to the ones we encounter today . . . .: quarrels and conflicts within the community of believers, the seductiveness of ersatz religious and philosophical doctrines, a superficial faith and a dissolute morality. St. Paul begins his letter by writing: "The word of the cross is folly to those who are perishing, but to us who are being saved it is the power of God" (1 Cor 1:18). Then, the Apostle shows the clear contrast between wisdom and folly, in God's way of thinking and in our own. . . . This wisdom, mysterious and hidden (cf. 1 Cor 2:7), has been revealed by the Spirit, because "the unspiritual man does not receive the gifts of the Spirit of God, for they are folly to him, and he is not able to understand them because they are spiritually discerned" (1 Cor 2:14).

The Spirit opens to human intelligence new horizons which transcend it and enable to perceive that the only true wisdom is found in the grandeur of Christ. For Christians, the Cross signifies God's wisdom and his infinite love revealed in the saving gift of Christ, crucified and risen for the life of the world, and in particular for the life of each and every one of you.

PRAYER VIGIL WITH THE YOUNG PEOPLE OF FRANCE,
SEPTEMBER 12, 2008

THE BAPTISM OF THE CHURCH

The Acts of the Apostles presents Pentecost . . . as the culmination of Jesus' entire mission. After his Resurrection, Jesus himself ordered the disciples to stay in Jerusalem, because, he said, "before many days you shall be baptized with the Holy Spirit" (Acts 1:5); and he added: "You shall receive power when the Holy Spirit has come upon you; and you shall be my witnesses in Jerusalem and in all Judea and Samaria and to the end of the earth" (Acts 1:8). Thus Pentecost is in a special way the Baptism of the Church which carries out her universal mission starting from the roads of Jerusalem with the miraculous preaching in humanity's different tongues. In this Baptism of the Holy Spirit the personal and community dimension, the "I" of the disciple and the "we" of the Church, are inseparable. The Holy Spirit consecrates the person and at the same time makes him or her a living member of the Mystical Body of Christ, sharing in the mission of witnessing to his love. And this takes place through the Sacraments of Christian initiation: Baptism and Confirmation. . . . Let us rediscover, dear brothers and sisters, the beauty of being baptized in the Holy Spirit; let us recover awareness of our Baptism and our Confirmation, ever timely sources of grace.

REGINA CAELI, MAY 11, 2008

MULTIPLYING BREAD FOR LIFE

*T*his is the beauty of the Christian truth: the Creator and Lord of all things makes himself a "grain of wheat" to be sown in our land, in the furrows of our history. He made himself bread to be broken, shared, eaten. He made himself our food to give us life, his same divine life. He was born in Bethlehem, which in Hebrew means "House of bread," and when he began to preach to the crowds he revealed that the Father had sent him into the world as "living bread come down from heaven," as the "bread of life."

The Eucharist is a school of charity and solidarity. The one who is nourished on the Bread of Christ cannot remain indifferent before the one who, even in our day, is deprived of daily bread. So many parents are barely able to obtain it for themselves and for their own children. It is an ever greater problem that the International Community has great difficulty in resolving. The Church not only prays "give us this day our daily bread," but, on the Lord's example, is committed in every way to "multiply the five loaves and the two fish" with numerous initiatives of human promotion and sharing, so that no one lacks what is necessary for life.

ANGELUS, MAY 25, 2008

THE APOSTLE OF MERCY

*L*ike St. Faustina, John Paul II in his turn made himself an apostle of Divine Mercy. In the evening of the unforgettable Saturday, April 2, 2005, when he closed his eyes on this world, it was precisely the eve of the Second Sunday of Easter [Divine Mercy Sunday], and many people noted the rare coincidence that combined the Marian dimension — the first Saturday of the month — and the dimension of Divine Mercy. This was in fact the core of John Paul II's long and multi-faceted Pontificate. The whole of his mission at the service of the truth about God and man and of peace in the world is summed up in this declaration, as he himself said in Krakow-Łagiewniki in 2002 when he inaugurated the large Shrine of Divine Mercy: "Apart from the mercy of God there is no other source of hope for mankind." John Paul II's message, like St. Faustina's, thus leads back to the Face of Christ, a supreme revelation of God's mercy. Constant contemplation of this Face is the legacy he bequeathed to us which we joyfully welcome and make our own.

REGINA CAELI, MARCH 30, 2008

THE DOUBTING THOMAS PARADOX

*W*e may all be tempted by the disbelief of Thomas. Suffering, evil, injustice, death, especially when it strikes the innocent such as children who are victims of war and terrorism, of sickness and hunger, does not all of this put our faith to the test? Paradoxically the disbelief of Thomas is most valuable to us in these cases because it helps to purify all false concepts of God and leads us to discover his true face: the face of a God who, in Christ, has taken upon himself the wounds of injured humanity. Thomas has received from the Lord, and has in turn transmitted to the Church, the gift of a faith put to the test by the passion and death of Jesus and confirmed by meeting him risen. His faith was almost dead but was born again thanks to his touching the wounds of Christ, those wounds that the Risen One did not hide but showed, and continues to point out to us in the trials and sufferings of every human being.

"By his wounds you have been healed" (1 Pet 2:24). This is the message Peter addressed to the early converts. Those wounds that, in the beginning were an obstacle for Thomas's faith, being a sign of Jesus' apparent failure, those same wounds have become in his encounter with the Risen One, signs of a victorious love. These wounds that Christ has received for love of us help us to understand who God is and to repeat: "My Lord and my God!"

Urbi et Orbi Message, Easter 2007

CATHOLIC SOCIAL CONSCIENCE

*T*he Church's social teaching argues on the basis of reason and natural law, namely, on the basis of what is in accord with the nature of every human being. It recognizes that it is not the Church's responsibility to make this teaching prevail in political life. Rather, the Church wishes to help form consciences in political life and to stimulate greater insight into the authentic requirements of justice as well as greater readiness to act accordingly, even when this might involve conflict with situations of personal interest. Building a just social and civil order, wherein each person receives what is his or her due, is an essential task which every generation must take up anew. As a political task, this cannot be the Church's immediate responsibility. Yet, since it is also a most important human responsibility, the Church is duty-bound to offer, through the purification of reason and through ethical formation, her own specific contribution toward understanding the requirements of justice and achieving them politically.

The Church cannot and must not take upon herself the political battle to bring about the most just society possible. She cannot and must not replace the State. Yet at the same time she cannot and must not remain on the sidelines in the fight for justice. She has to play her part through rational argument and she has to reawaken the spiritual energy without which justice, which always demands sacrifice, cannot prevail and prosper.

DEUS CARITAS EST, 28A

THE BEAUTY OF THE LITURGY

*T*his relationship between creed and worship is evidenced in a particular way by the rich theological and liturgical category of beauty. Like the rest of Christian Revelation, the liturgy is inherently linked to beauty: it is *veritatis splendor.* The liturgy is a radiant expression of the paschal mystery, in which Christ draws us to himself and calls us to communion. As St. Bonaventure would say, in Jesus we contemplate beauty and splendor at their source. This is no mere aestheticism, but the concrete way in which the truth of God's love in Christ encounters us, attracts us, and delights us, enabling us to emerge from ourselves and drawing us toward our true vocation, which is love. God allows himself to be glimpsed first in creation, in the beauty and harmony of the cosmos (cf. Wis 13:5; Rom 1:19-20). . . . In the New Testament this epiphany of beauty reaches definitive fulfillment in God's revelation in Jesus Christ: Christ is the full manifestation of the glory of God. . . .

The beauty of the liturgy is part of this mystery; it is a sublime expression of God's glory and, in a certain sense, a glimpse of heaven on earth. The memorial of Jesus' redemptive sacrifice contains something of that beauty which Peter, James, and John beheld when the Master, making his way to Jerusalem, was transfigured before their eyes (cf. Mk 9:2). Beauty, then, is not mere decoration, but rather an essential element of the liturgical action, since it is an attribute of God himself and his revelation.

SACRAMENTUM CARITATIS, 35

THE CRUCIFIED AND RISEN LORD

*S*t. Paul's pastoral and theological intention was so focused on fostering the nascent communities that it came naturally to him to concentrate completely on the proclamation of Jesus Christ as "Lord," alive now and present now among his followers. . . . For the Apostle the Resurrection is not an event in itself, separate from death: the Risen One is always the One who has first been crucified. Even as the Risen One he bears his wounds: the Passion is present in him and we can say . . . that he is the Suffering One until the end of the world, while at the same time being the Risen One and living with us and for us. Paul had understood this identification of the Risen One with the Crucified Christ at the encounter on the road to Damascus: at that moment it was clearly revealed to him that the Crucified One is the Risen One and the Risen One is the Crucified One, who asks Paul: "Why do you persecute me?" (Acts 9:4). Paul is persecuting Christ in the Church and then realizes that the Cross is not "accursed by God" (Deut 21:23), but is also the sacrifice for our redemption.

GENERAL AUDIENCE, OCTOBER 22, 2008

ST. LAWRENCE AND THE CHURCH'S TREASURES

*C*haritable activity on behalf of the poor and suffering was naturally an essential part of the Church of Rome from the very beginning, based on the principles of Christian life given in the Acts of the Apostles. It found a vivid expression in the case of the deacon Lawrence (d. 258). The dramatic description of Lawrence's martyrdom was known to St. Ambrose (d. 397), and it provides a fundamentally authentic picture of the saint. As the one responsible for the care of the poor in Rome, Lawrence had been given a period of time, after the capture of the Pope and of Lawrence's fellow deacons, to collect the treasures of the Church and hand them over to the civil authorities. He distributed to the poor whatever funds were available and then presented to the authorities the poor themselves as the real treasure of the Church. Whatever historical reliability one attributes to these details, Lawrence has always remained present in the Church's memory as a great exponent of ecclesial charity.

Deus Caritas Est, **23**

THE NEW IDOLATRY

*W*hat can be said of the fact that, in the current consumers' society, profit and success have become the new idols before which so many prostrate themselves?

The consequence is that it has brought us to give value solely to who, as is often said, "is lucky" and has "fame," certainly not those who must laboriously battle with life each day.

Possession of material goods and applause of the masses have replaced the work on oneself that serves to temper the spirit and form an authentic personality. One risks being superficial, taking dangerous short-cuts in the search for success, thus consigning life to experiences that give immediate satisfaction, but are in themselves precarious and misleading.

The tendency toward individualism is growing, and when one is concentrated only on oneself, one inevitably becomes fragile; the capacity to listen is weakened, which is an indispensable stage in understanding others and working together.

ADDRESS TO THE YOUTH OF SARDINIA, SEPTEMBER 7, 2008

A COMMON HOPE

At the Passover Sèder you recall the holy patriarchs Abraham, Isaac, and Jacob, and the holy women of Israel, Sarah, Rebecca, Rachael, and Leah, the beginning of the long line of sons and daughters of the Covenant. With the passing of time the Covenant assumes an ever more universal value, as the promise made to Abraham takes form: "by you all the families of the earth shall bless themselves" (Gen 12:3). Indeed, according to the prophet Isaiah . . . : "Many peoples will come and say: 'Come, let us go up to the mountain of the LORD, to the house of the God of Jacob; that he may teach us his ways and that we may walk in his paths'" (Is 2:3).

Within this eschatological horizon is offered a real prospect of universal brotherhood on the path of justice and peace, preparing the way of the Lord (cf. Is 62:10).

Christians and Jews share this hope; we are in fact, as the prophets say, "prisoners of hope" (Zech 9:12). This bond permits us Christians to celebrate alongside you, though in our own way, the Passover of Christ's death and resurrection, which we see as inseparable from your own, for Jesus himself said: "salvation is from the Jews" (Jn 4:22). Our Easter and your Pesah, while distinct and different, unite us in our common hope centered on God and his mercy. They urge us to cooperate with each other and with all men and women of goodwill to make this a better world for all as we await the fulfillment of God's promises.

MESSAGE TO THE JEWISH COMMUNITY
ON THE FEAST OF PESAH,
APRIL 14, 2008

THE HYMN TO JESUS' HUMILITY

$\mathcal{L}$ et us [consider] the hymn in the Letter to the Philippians (2:5-11). This text's structure is in three strophes, which illustrate the high points on the journey undertaken by Christ. His preexistence is expressed by the words: "though he was in the form of God, [he] did not count equality with God a thing to be grasped" (Phil 2:6). Then comes the Son's voluntary self-abasement in the second strophe: "emptied himself, taking the form of a servant" (v. 7), to the point of humbling himself and "[becoming] obedient unto death, even death on a cross" (v. 8). The third strophe of the hymn proclaims the Father's response to the Son's humbling of himself: "Therefore God has highly exalted him and bestowed on him the name which is above every name" (v. 9). What is striking is the contrast between the radical humbling of himself and his subsequent glorification in the glory of God. It is obvious that this second strophe is in contrast with the claim of Adam, who wanted to make a God of himself, and in contrast with the act of the builders of the tower of Babel, who wanted to construct a bridge to Heaven and make themselves divinities. However, this initiative of pride ended in self-destruction: this is not the way to Heaven, to true happiness, to God. The gesture of the Son of God is exactly the opposite: not pride but humility, which is the fulfillment of love, and love is divine.

General Audience, October 22, 2008

CHARISMS FOR RELIGIOUS COMMUNITIES

*R*eligious Sisters, Brothers, and Priests contribute greatly to the mission of the Church. Their prophetic witness is marked by a profound conviction of the primacy with which the Gospel shapes Christian life and transforms society. Today, I wish to draw your attention to the positive spiritual renewal which Congregations are undertaking in relation to their charism. The word charism means a gift freely and graciously given. Charisms are bestowed by the Holy Spirit, who inspires founders and foundresses and shapes Congregations with a subsequent spiritual heritage. The wondrous array of charisms proper to each Religious Institute is an extraordinary spiritual treasury. Indeed, the history of the Church is perhaps most beautifully portrayed through the history of her schools of spirituality, most of which stem from the saintly lives of founders and foundresses. Through the discovery of charisms, which yield such a breadth of spiritual wisdom, I am sure that some of you young people will be drawn to a life of apostolic or contemplative service. Do not be shy to speak with Religious Brothers, Sisters, or Priests about the charism and spirituality of their Congregation. No perfect community exists, but it is fidelity to a founding charism, not to particular individuals, that the Lord calls you to discern. Have courage! You too can make your life a gift of self for the love of the Lord Jesus and, in him, of every member of the human family (cf. *Vita Consecrata*, 3).

MEETING WITH YOUNG PEOPLE AND SEMINARIANS
AT SAINT JOSEPH SEMINARY, YONKERS, NEW YORK,
APRIL 19, 2008

THE CHARACTERISTICS OF AN APOSTLE

Though he did not belong to the group of the Twelve, called by Jesus during his ministry, Paul nevertheless claims the title for himself because he was chosen and transformed by the grace of God and shared the three principal characteristics of the true apostle. The first is to have seen the Lord (cf. 1 Cor 9:1) and to have been called by him. One becomes an apostle by divine vocation, not by personal choice. The second characteristic also underlines the divine initiative: an apostle is someone who is sent and therefore acts and speaks as a delegate of Christ, placed totally at his service. The third characteristic is dedication to the work of proclaiming the Gospel and founding Christian communities. St. Paul can point to his many trials and sufferings that speak clearly of his courageous dedication to the mission (cf. 2 Cor 11:23-28). In this context he sees an identification between the life of the apostle and the Gospel that he preaches; the apostle himself is despised when the Gospel is rejected. St. Paul was steadfast in his many difficulties and persecutions, sustained above all by the unfailing love of Christ (cf. Rom 8:35-39). May the example of his apostolic zeal inspire and encourage us today!

GENERAL AUDIENCE, SEPTEMBER 10, 2008

THE SUPREME SIGN OF GOD'S LOVE

Consider the central place of the Cross of Jesus Christ in St. Paul's preaching. Paul's encounter with the glorified Lord on the way to Damascus convinced him that Jesus had died and risen for him and for all. The mystery of the Cross showed him the power of God's merciful and saving love. As Paul told the Corinthians, he came not to preach in lofty words or wisdom, but to proclaim "Jesus Christ, and him crucified" (cf. 1 Cor 2:2). The Cross, which seems a stumbling block to Jews and folly to Gentiles, is the revelation of God's wisdom and strength. As the supreme sign of God's love for sinful humanity, the Cross invites us to that true wisdom which accepts the free gift of God's merciful and saving love. On the Cross Christ gave himself up for our sins (cf. Gal 1:4), becoming a sacrifice of atonement in his own blood (cf. Rom 3:25). For Paul, faith in the crucified Lord thus calls us to crucify our own flesh with its desires, in order to share in Christ's death and resurrection (cf. Gal 5:24). In accepting the weakness of the Cross, we experience the power of God's love for us.

GENERAL AUDIENCE, OCTOBER 29, 2008

THE ILLUSION OF MATERIALISM

*F*or an affluent society, a further obstacle to an encounter with the living God lies in the subtle influence of materialism, which can all too easily focus the attention on the hundredfold, which God promises now in this time, at the expense of the eternal life which he promises in the age to come (cf. Mk 10:30). People today need to be reminded of the ultimate purpose of their lives. They need to recognize that implanted within them is a deep thirst for God. They need to be given opportunities to drink from the wells of his infinite love. It is easy to be entranced by the almost unlimited possibilities that science and technology place before us; it is easy to make the mistake of thinking we can obtain by our own efforts the fulfillment of our deepest needs. This is an illusion. Without God, who alone bestows upon us what we by ourselves cannot attain (cf. *Spe Salvi*, 31), our lives are ultimately empty. People need to be constantly reminded to cultivate a relationship with him who came that we might have life in abundance (cf. Jn 10:10). The goal of all our pastoral and catechetical work, the object of our preaching, and the focus of our sacramental ministry should be to help people establish and nurture that living relationship with "Christ Jesus our hope" (1 Tim 1:1).

MEETING WITH THE BISHOPS OF THE
UNITED STATES OF AMERICA, APRIL 16, 2008

THE MISSION OF YOUTH

There are those who think that to present the precious treasure of faith to people who do not share it means being intolerant toward them, but this is not the case, because to present Christ is not to impose Him (cf. *Evangelii Nuntiandi*, 80). Moreover, two thousand years ago twelve Apostles gave their lives to make Christ known and loved. Throughout the centuries since then, the Gospel has continued to spread by means of men and women inspired by that same missionary fervor. Today too there is a need for disciples of Christ who give unstintingly of their time and energy to serve the Gospel. There is a need for young people who will allow God's love to burn within them and who will respond generously to his urgent call, just as many young blesseds and saints did in the past and also in more recent times. In particular, I assure you that the Spirit of Jesus today is inviting you young people to be bearers of the good news of Jesus to your contemporaries. The difficulty that adults undoubtedly find in approaching the sphere of youth in a comprehensible and convincing way could be a sign with which the Spirit is urging you young people to take this task upon yourselves. You know the ideals, the language, and also the wounds, the expectations, and at the same time the desire for goodness felt by your contemporaries.

MESSAGE TO THE YOUNG PEOPLE OF THE WORLD ON THE OCCASION OF THE 23RD WORLD YOUTH DAY, 2008

TWO WAYS OF KNOWING JESUS

*S*t. Paul himself distinguishes between two ways of knowing Jesus, and more generally, two ways of knowing a person. He writes in his Second Letter to the Corinthians: "from now on, therefore, we regard no one according to the flesh; even though we once regarded Christ according to the flesh, we regard him thus no longer" (5:16). Knowing "from a human point of view," in the manner of the flesh, means knowing solely in an external way, by means of external criteria: one may have seen a person various times and hence be familiar with his features and various characteristics of his behavior: how he speaks, how he moves, etc. Although one may know someone in this way, nevertheless one does not really know him, one does not know the essence of the person. Only with the heart does one truly know a person. Indeed, the Pharisees and the Sadducees were externally acquainted with Jesus, they learned his teaching and knew many details about him but they did not know him in his truth. . . . On the other hand, the Twelve, thanks to the friendship that calls the heart into question, have at least understood in substance and begun to discover who Jesus is. This different manner of knowing still exists today: there are learned people who know many details about Jesus and simple people who have no knowledge of these details but have known him in his truth: "Heart speaks to heart."

General Audience, October 8, 2008

ZEALOUS CONCERN FOR MIGRANTS

[St. Paul's] life and his preaching were wholly directed to making Jesus known and loved by all, for all persons are called to become a single people in him.

This is the mission of the Church and of every baptized person in our time too, even in the era of globalization; a mission that with attentive pastoral solicitude is also directed to the variegated universe of migrants — students far from home, immigrants, refugees, displaced people, evacuees — including, for example, the victims of modern forms of slavery and of human trafficking. Today too the message of salvation must be presented with the same approach as that of the Apostle to the Gentiles, taking into account the different social and cultural situations and special difficulties of each one as a consequence of his or her condition as a migrant or itinerant person. I express the wish that every Christian community may feel the same apostolic zeal as St. Paul who, although he was proclaiming to all the saving love of the Father (cf. Rom 8:15-16; Gal 4:6) to "win the more" (1 Cor 9:19) for Christ, made himself weak "to the weak . . . all things to all men so that [he] might by all means save some" (1 Cor 9:22). May his example also be an incentive for us to show solidarity to these brothers and sisters of ours and to promote, in every part of the world and by every means, peaceful coexistence among different races, cultures, and religions.

MESSAGE FOR THE 95TH WORLD DAY
OF MIGRANTS AND REFUGEES, 2009

THE WORK OF JESUS

$\mathcal{I}$n the liturgy we find the whole Church at prayer. The word liturgy means the participation of God's people in "the work of Christ the Priest and of His Body which is the Church" *(Sacrosanctum Concilium*, 7). What is that work? First of all it refers to Christ's Passion, his Death and Resurrection, and his Ascension — what we call the Paschal Mystery. It also refers to the celebration of the liturgy itself. The two meanings are in fact inseparably linked because this "work of Jesus" is the real content of the liturgy. Through the liturgy, the "work of Jesus" is continually brought into contact with history; with our lives in order to shape them. Here we catch another glimpse of the grandeur of our Christian faith. Whenever you gather for Mass, when you go to Confession, whenever you celebrate any of the sacraments, Jesus is at work. Through the Holy Spirit, he draws you to himself, into his sacrificial love of the Father which becomes love for all. We see then that the Church's liturgy is a ministry of hope for humanity. Your faithful participation, is an active hope which helps to keep the world — saints and sinners alike — open to God; this is the truly human hope we offer everyone (cf. *Spe Salvi*, 34).

MEETING WITH YOUNG PEOPLE AND SEMINARIANS
AT SAINT JOSEPH SEMINARY, YONKERS, NEW YORK, APRIL 19, 2008

THE SEARCH FOR A SAVIOR

*I*s the humanity of our time still waiting for a Savior? One has the feeling that many consider God as foreign to their own interests. Apparently, they do not need him. They live as though he did not exist and, worse still, as though he were an "obstacle" to remove in order to fulfill themselves. Even among believers — we are sure of it — some let themselves be attracted by enticing dreams and distracted by misleading doctrines that suggest deceptive short-cuts to happiness.

Yet, despite its contradictions, worries, and tragedies, and per-haps precisely because of them, humanity today seeks a path of renewal, of salvation, it seeks a Savior and awaits, sometimes uncon-sciously, the coming of the Savior who renews the world and our life, the coming of Christ, the one true Redeemer of man and of the whole of man.

Of course, false prophets continue to propose a salvation "at a cheap price," that always ends by producing searing disappointments.

The history of the past 50 years itself demonstrates this search for a Savior "at a cheap price" and highlights all the disappointments that have derived from it. It is the task of us Christians, with the witness of our life, to spread the truth of Christmas which Christ brings to every man and woman of good will.

GENERAL AUDIENCE, DECEMBER 20, 2006

POPE PIUS XII AND THE JEWS

*T*he war highlighted the love Pope Pius XII felt for his "beloved Rome," a love attested by the intense charitable work he promoted on behalf of the persecuted, without distinction of religion, race, nationality, or political affiliation. . . . How can we forget his Christmas Radio Message in December 1942? His voice broken by emotion, he deplored the situation of "hundreds of thousands of men and women who, without any fault of their own, sometimes only because of their nationality or race, have been consigned to death or to a slow decline" (AAS, xxxv, 1943, p. 23), with a clear reference to the deportation and extermination of the Jews. He often acted secretly and silently because, in the light of the practical situations of that complex period of history, he foresaw that only in this way could he avoid the worst and save the greatest possible number of Jews. Numerous and unanimous attestations of gratitude for his interventions were addressed to him at the end of the war, as well as at the time of his death, from the highest authorities of the Jewish world such as, for example, Israel's Minister for Foreign Affairs Golda Meir, who wrote: "When fearful martyrdom came to our people, the voice of the Pope was raised for its victims. The life of our times was enriched by a voice speaking out about great moral truths above the tumult of daily conflict," and concluded with emotion, "We mourn a great Servant of peace."

HOMILY, OCTOBER 9, 2008

THE MASS, A PATTERN FOR OUR LIFE

*T*he Eucharist is also a model of the Christian journey which must shape our existence. It is Christ who convokes us to gather together, to constitute the Church, his Body, in the midst of the world. To be admitted to the twofold table of the Word and the Bread, we must first receive God's forgiveness, the gift which . . . restores the divine image within us. . . . Then, just as in Luke's Gospel he addressed Simon the Pharisee, Jesus continuously addresses us through Scripture: "I have something to say to you" (7:40). Indeed, every word of Scripture is a word of life for us that we must listen to with great attention. In a particular way, the Gospel constitutes the heart of the Christian message, the total revelation of the divine mysteries. . . . During the consecration, an especially important moment of the Eucharist because in it we commemorate Christ's sacrifice, you are called to contemplate the Lord Jesus, like St. Thomas: "My Lord and my God" (Jn 20:28). After receiving the Word of God, after having been nourished by his Body, let yourselves be inwardly transformed and receive your mission from him. Indeed, he sends you into the world to be messengers of his peace and witnesses of his message of love. Do not be afraid to proclaim Christ to the young people of your age. Show them that Christ does not hamper your life or your freedom; show them that, on the contrary, he gives you true life, that he sets you free to fight evil and to make something beautiful of your life.

VIDEO MESSAGE TO YOUNG PARTICIPANTS IN THE 49TH
INTERNATIONAL EUCHARISTIC CONGRESS IN QUÉBEC, CANADA,
JUNE 21, 2008

SCRIPTURE LIGHTS UP OUR PATH

*I*t is not easy to recognize and find authentic happiness in this world in which we live, where people are often held captive by the current ways of thinking. They may think they are "free," but they are being led astray and become lost amid the errors or illusions of aberrant ideologies. "Freedom itself needs to be set free" (cf. *Veritatis Splendor*, 86), and the darkness in which humankind is groping needs to be illuminated. Jesus taught us how this can be done: "If you continue in my word, you are truly my disciples, and you will know the truth, and the truth will make you free" (Jn 8:31-32). The incarnate Word, Word of Truth, makes us free and directs our freedom toward the good. My dear young friends, meditate often on the word of God, and allow the Holy Spirit to be your teacher. You will then discover that God's way of thinking is not the same as that of humankind's. You will find yourselves led to contemplate the real God and to read the events of history through his eyes. You will savor in fullness the joy that is born of truth. . . . The loving presence of God, through his word, is the lamp that dispels the darkness of fear and lights up the path even when times are most difficult.

MESSAGE TO THE YOUTH OF THE WORLD ON THE
OCCASION OF THE 21ST WORLD YOUTH DAY,
APRIL 9, 2006

UNENDING LOVE

*T*hus the love of Christ is the love that "never ends" (1 Cor 13:8), the spiritual energy that unites all who share in the same sacrifice and are nourished by the one Bread, broken for the world's salvation. Indeed, how is it possible to communicate with the Lord if we do not communicate with one another? How can we present ourselves divided, distant from one another, at God's altar? May this altar on which the Lord's sacrifice will shortly be renewed, be a constant invitation to you, dear brothers and sisters, to love; you will always approach it disposed to accept love in your hearts, to spread it, and to receive and grant forgiveness.

HOMILY, SEPTEMBER 21, 2008

THE NAME ABOVE EVERY OTHER NAME

*I*n truth, the Risen Jesus Christ, "exalted above every other name," is at the center of every reflection Paul makes. Christ, for the Apostle, is the criterion for evaluating events and things, the goal of every effort that he makes to proclaim the Gospel, the great passion that sustains his footsteps on the roads of the world. And this is a real and living Christ: "Christ," Paul says, "who loved me and gave himself for me" (Gal 2:20). This person who loves me, with whom I can speak, who listens to me and answers me, this is truly the starting point for understanding the world and finding the way through history.

GENERAL AUDIENCE, OCTOBER 22, 2008

THE ASSURANCE OF
THE ASCENSION

*I*n his farewell discourses to the disciples, Jesus stressed the importance of his "return to the Father," the culmination of his whole mission: indeed, he came into the world to bring man back to God, not on the ideal level — like a philosopher or a master of wisdom — but really, like a shepherd who wants to lead his sheep back to the fold. This "exodus" toward the heavenly Homeland which Jesus lived in the first person, he faced solely for us. It was for our sake that he came down from Heaven and for our sake that he ascended to it, after making himself in all things like men, humbling himself even to death on a cross and after having touched the abyss of the greatest distance from God. For this very reason the Father was pleased with him and "highly exalted" him (Phil 2:9), restoring to him the fullness of his glory, but now with our humanity. God in man — man in God: this is even now a reality, not a theoretical truth. Therefore, Christian hope, founded on Christ, is not an illusion but, as the Letter to the Hebrews says, "we have this as a sure and steadfast anchor of the soul" (Heb 6:19), an anchor that penetrates Heaven where Christ has gone before us.

REGINA CAELI, MAY 4, 2008

YOU ARE WHAT YOU RECEIVE

The "subject" of the liturgy's intrinsic beauty is Christ himself, risen and glorified in the Holy Spirit, who includes the Church in his work. Here we can recall an evocative phrase of St. Augustine which strikingly describes this dynamic of faith proper to the Eucharist. The great Bishop of Hippo, speaking specifically of the eucharistic mystery, stresses the fact that Christ assimilates us to himself: "The bread you see on the altar, sanctified by the word of God, is the body of Christ. The chalice, or rather, what the chalice contains, sanctified by the word of God, is the blood of Christ. In these signs, Christ the Lord willed to entrust to us his body and the blood which he shed for the forgiveness of our sins. If you have received them properly, you yourselves are what you have received." Consequently, "not only have we become Christians, we have become Christ himself." We can thus contemplate God's mysterious work, which brings about a profound unity between ourselves and the Lord Jesus: "one should not believe that Christ is in the head but not in the body; rather he is complete in the head and in the body."

SACRAMENTUM CARITATIS, 36

APPLYING CHRIST'S VICTORY

*I*f, to save us, the Son of God had to suffer and die on the Cross, it was certainly not by a cruel design of the heavenly Father. The reason is the gravity of the illness from which he came to heal us: it was such a serious, mortal disease that it required all his Blood. Indeed, it was with his death and Resurrection that Jesus defeated sin and death and re-established God's lordship. Yet the battle is not over. Evil exists and resists in every generation, as we know, in our day too. What are the horrors of war, violence to the innocent, the wretchedness and injustice unleashed against the weak other than the opposition of evil to the Kingdom of God? And how is it possible to respond to so much wickedness except with the unarmed and disarming power of love that conquers hatred and of life that has no fear of death? It is the same mysterious power that Jesus used, at the cost of being misunderstood and abandoned by many of his own.

Dear brothers and sisters, in order to bring the work of salvation fully to completion, the Redeemer continues to associate to himself and his mission men and women who are prepared to take up their cross and follow him.

ANGELUS, AUGUST 31, 2008

A LUMINOUS SIGN

*S*ome people today live as if they never had to die or as if, with death, everything were over; others, who hold that man is the one and only author of his own destiny, behave as though God did not exist, and at times they even reach the point of denying that there is room for him in our world.

Yet, the great breakthroughs of technology and science that have considerably improved humanity's condition leave unresolved the deepest searchings of the human soul.

Only openness to the mystery of God, who is Love, can quench the thirst for truth and happiness in our hearts; only the prospect of eternity can give authentic value to historical events and especially to the mystery of human frailty, suffering, and death.

By contemplating Mary in heavenly glory, we understand that the earth is not the definitive homeland for us either, and that if we live with our gaze fixed on eternal goods we will one day share in this same glory and the earth will become more beautiful.

Consequently, we must not lose our serenity and peace even amid the thousands of daily difficulties. The luminous sign of Our

Lady taken up into Heaven shines out even more brightly when sad shadows of suffering and violence seem to loom on the horizon.

General Audience, August 16, 2006

GIFT AND TASK

*S*acred Scripture affirms that "God created man in his own image, in the image of God he created him; male and female he created them" (Gen 1:27). As one created in the image of God, each individual human being has the dignity of a person; he or she is not just something, but someone, capable of self-knowledge, self-possession, free self-giving, and entering into communion with others. At the same time, each person is called, by grace, to a covenant with the Creator, called to offer him a response of faith and love that no other creature can give in his place. From this supernatural perspective, one can understand the task entrusted to human beings to mature in the ability to love and to contribute to the progress of the world, renewing it in justice and in peace. In a striking synthesis, St. Augustine teaches that "God created us without our aid; but he did not choose to save us without our aid." Consequently all human beings have the duty to cultivate an awareness of this twofold aspect of gift and task.

MESSAGE FOR THE CELEBRATION OF THE
WORLD DAY OF PEACE 2006

QUENCHING HUMANITY'S THIRST

*I*n persevering prayer, in fervent meditation on God's Word, in obedience to the Magisterium of the Church, in the dignified celebration of the Sacraments, and in witnessing to brotherly charity, may you find the strength you need in order to identify with Christ's sentiments and thus to be his coherent and generous disciples, proclaiming with your personal example that Christ is the Son of God, the Redeemer of man, the solid rock on which to build our existence. May you drink the life-giving water that flows from the Savior's side and that satiates with its crystal freshness all who thirst for justice, peace, and truth, those who are oppressed by being locked in by sin, by the tarnish of relativism, by the hardness of hearts, and by the obscurity of violence. May you feel Christ's consolation and offer the balm of his love to the troubled, to those oppressed by suffering or who have been wounded by the coldness of indifferentism or the scourge of corruption. These challenges demand that individualism and isolation be overcome. They require the strengthening of a sense of ecclesial belonging and loyal collaboration with Pastors, in order to form Christian communities that are prayerful, harmonious, fraternal, and missionary.

MESSAGE TO HIS EMINENCE CARDINAL ANTONIO JOSÉ
GONZÁLEZ ZUMÁRRAGA, AUGUST 12, 2008

TAKE THE LORD'S HAND

*A*fter the multiplication of the loaves, the Lord withdraws to the mountain to be alone with the Father. In the meantime, the disciples are on the lake and with their poor little boat are endeavoring in vain to stand up to a contrary wind. To the Evangelist this episode may have seemed an image of the Church of his time: like the small barque which was the Church of that period, he found himself buffeted by the contrary wind of history, and it may have seemed that the Lord had forgotten him. We too can see this as an image of the Church of our time which in many parts of the earth finds herself struggling to make headway in spite of the contrary wind, and it seems the Lord is very remote. But the Gospel gives us an answer, consolation, and encouragement, and at the same time points out a path to us. It tells us, in fact: yes, it is true, the Lord is with the Father but for this very reason he is not distant but sees everyone, for whoever is with God does not go away but is close to his neighbor. And, in fact, the Lord sees them and at the proper time comes toward them. And when Peter, who was going to meet him, risks drowning, the Lord takes him by the hand and brings him to safety on the boat. The Lord is continuously holding out his hand to us too. . . . And only if we take the Lord's hand, if we let ourselves be guided by him, will the path we take be right and good.

ANGELUS, AUGUST 10, 2008

DON'T BE AFRAID

*I*n the face of the broad and diversified panorama of human fears, the Word of God is clear: those who "fear" God "are not afraid." Fear of God, which the Scriptures define as "the beginning of knowledge" (Prov 1:7) coincides with faith in him, with sacred respect for his authority over life and the world.

To be without "fear of God" is equivalent to putting ourselves in his place, to feeling we ourselves are lords of good and evil, of life and death. Instead, those who fear God feel within them the safety that an infant in his mother's arms feels (cf. Ps 130:2). Those who fear God are tranquil even in the midst of storms for, as Jesus revealed to us, God is a Father full of mercy and goodness. Those who love him are not afraid: "There is no fear in love," the Apostle John wrote, "but perfect love casts out fear. For fear has to do with punishment, and he who fears is not perfected in love" (1 Jn 4:18). Believers, therefore, are not afraid of anything because they know they are in the hands of God, they know that it is not evil and the irrational which have the last word, but rather that the one Lord of the world and of love is Christ, the Word of God Incarnate, who loved us to the point of sacrificing himself for us, dying on the Cross for our salvation.

ANGELUS, JUNE 22, 2008

ABOUT POPE BENEDICT XVI

*J*oseph Cardinal Ratzinger was elected by the College of Cardinals to the papacy on April 19, 2005. He took the name Benedict after two great figures: St. Benedict of Nursia, whose model of monastic life helped rebuild European culture after the collapse of the Roman Empire; and Pope Benedict XV, who was committed to bring peace to a Europe again torn by war during World War I.

Joseph Ratzinger was born on April 16, 1927, on Holy Saturday. In his youth, he was exposed to the horrors of Nazi Germany, which temporarily halted his pursuit of the priesthood. After the war, in 1951, his brother Georg and he were ordained on the same day. Other milestones in his life include:

- 1951-77 — Served as professor of theology at German universities
- 1962-65 — Attended sessions of the Second Vatican Council as a theological advisor
- 1977-81 — Served as Archbishop of Munich and Freising
- 1981-2005 — Served as Prefect of the Congregation for the Doctrine of the Faith, the office responsible for safeguarding the faithful teaching of the Gospel throughout the Church

- April 19, 2005 — Elected the 265th Pope of the Catholic Church at the age of 78

Pope Benedict is the author of numerous books on theology, Scripture, liturgy, and the life of the Christian in the modern world. His book *Jesus of Nazareth*, published in the spring of 2007, has sold millions of copies and been translated into thirty-two languages.

As pope, Benedict XVI dedicates himself to the responsibilities of his office: appointing and meeting with bishops, meeting with world leaders, canonizing saints, preaching, and teaching. He has published two encyclicals, one on love (*Deus Caritas*, 2005) and the other on hope (*Spe Salvi*, 2007).

A Pope's primary responsibility is preserving the truth of the Gospel Jesus taught in the modern world. But popes are individuals, with their own particular gifts and emphases in thinking. As Pope Benedict XVI shares the Gospel, his homilies, speeches, encyclicals, and books reflect certain important themes he clearly believes are important for the world to take to heart:

- **Faith is a life-giving friendship with Christ.**

   "If we let Christ into our lives, we lose nothing, nothing, absolutely nothing of what makes life free, beautiful, and great. No! Only in this friendship are the doors of life opened wide. Only in this friendship is the great potential of human existence truly revealed. Only in this friendship do we experience beauty and liberation." (Inaugural Mass homily, April 24, 2005)

- **A Christian loves and serves as Jesus did.**

"In God and with God, I love even the person whom I do not like or even know. This can only take place on the basis of an intimate encounter with God, an encounter which has become a communion of will, even affecting my feelings. Then I learn to look on this other person not simply with my eyes and my feelings, but from the perspective of Jesus Christ. His friend is my friend." (*Deus Caritas Est*, 5)

- **Faith and Reason are not opposed.**

"Faith presupposes reason and perfects it, and reason, enlightened by faith, finds the strength to rise to knowledge of God and spiritual realities." (Angelus, January 28, 2007)

- **Living a life of faith is hard — but worth the effort.**

"We all know that to reach a goal in a sport or in one's profession, discipline and sacrifices are required; but then, by reaching a desired goal, it is all crowned with success. Life itself is like this. In other words, becoming men and women according to Jesus' plan demands sacrifices, but these are by no means negative; on the contrary, they are a help in living as people with new hearts, in living a truly human and happy life." (Responses to questions of young people, Rome, April 6, 2006)

In his visit to the United States in April of 2008, Pope Benedict XVI enjoined American Catholics to:

- **Appreciate American Catholic roots.** Speaking of the impressive growth which God has given the Church in the United States in the past 200 years, he said, "On these solid foundations the future of the Church in America must, even now, begin to rise!"

- **Make education a priority.** He particularly stressed the importance of knowing the Faith and that religious education for children, youth, and adults must be "maintained and expanded" — "The challenges confronting us require a comprehensive and sound instruction in the truths of the faith."

- **Live our Faith every day.** He called us to form a "mindset . . . which is genuinely Catholic, confident in the profound harmony of faith and reason, and prepared to bring the richness of faith's vision to bear on the urgent issues which affect the future of American society."

- **Defend the weakest among us.** He noted that we must care for those who cannot defend themselves because we believe in the "inalienable dignity and rights of each man, woman, and child in our world — including the most defenseless of all human beings, the unborn child in the mother's womb."

- **Seek unity.** He expressed sorrow for the divisions within the Church and called on Catholics to "reaffirm their unity in the apostolic Faith" so we move beyond sterile divisions, disagreements, and preconceptions and listen to the voice of the Spirit who is guiding the Church into a future of hope.
- **Make Christ the center of our lives.** He challenged listeners to turn to Christ. The Church's mission is ultimately one of evangelization, introducing people to Christ's "transforming love and truth." This is where renewal begins. "Our most urgent challenge is to communicate the joy born of faith and the experience of God's love."

In the homily at his Inaugural Mass, Pope Benedict asked for our prayers:

> My dear friends — at this moment I can only say: pray for me, that I may learn to love the Lord more and more. Pray for me, that I may learn to love his flock more and more — in other words, you, the holy Church, each one of you and all of you together. Pray for me, that I may not flee for fear of the wolves. Let us pray for one another, that the Lord will carry us and that we will learn to carry one another.

A PRAYER FOR THE POPE

Lord, source of eternal life and truth, give to Your shepherd, the Pope, a spirit of courage and right judgment, a spirit of knowledge and love.

By governing with fidelity those entrusted to his care may he, as successor to the apostle Peter and vicar of Christ, build Your church into a sacrament of unity, love, and peace for all the world.

We ask this through our Lord Jesus Christ, Your Son, Who lives and reigns with You and the Holy Spirit, one God, forever and ever. Amen.